CREATIVE THINKING OF SCHOOL STUDENTS

CREATIVE THINKING OF SCHOOL STUDENTS

By

Sarvepalli Sivaram Prasad
M.Ed., M.Phil.
Teacher
Municipal High School
Nellore, Andhra Pradesh
ssur_143@yahoo.com

Editor

Dr. Digumarti Bhaskara Rao
M.Sc., M.A., M.A., M.Ed., Ph.D.
Reader & Research Director
R.V.R. College of Education
Guntur – 522006, A.P.
digumartibhaskararao@rediffmail.com

DISCOVERY PUBLISHING HOUSE PVT. LTD.
NEW DELHI-110 002

First Published – 2009

Reprinted – 2016

ISBN: 978-81-8356-426-7

Creative Thinking of School Students

Published by:

DISCOVERY PUBLISHING HOUSE PVT. LTD.
4383/4B, Ansari Road, Darya Ganj
New Delhi-110 002 (India)
Phone: +91-11-23279245, 43596064-65
Fax: +91-11-23253475
E-mail: discoverypublishinghouse@gmail.com
sales@discoverypublishinggroup.com
web: www.discoverypublishinggroup.com

Printed at:
Infinity Imaging Systems
Delhi

dedicated

to

Mr. Chandra Sarat Chandra

Microsoft Corporation

United States of America

&

Ms. Harshitha Digumarthi

Bank of America

United States of America

in recognition of their

public spirited service

PREFACE

Creative thinking is one of the key sources for the development of human civilisation. Almost all activities of mankind are one way or the other concerned to creative thinking and out of that creative thinking only the mankind is surviving with all convenience and comfort to the core. Creative thinking is a unique psychic wonder, which is altering the history of man time and again through reshaping man's imaginary world with all newness.

Creative thinking can be developed through strategies like encouragement, developing basics skills, encouraging to take risks, self management, self competition, discovery, exploration, knowledge, performance, motivation, confidence, mastery, etc., which can be taken care of at home and in school.

The present study is intended to find out the level of creative thinking of secondary school students. The secondary school students are holding a high level of creative thinking. The gender of the student, the locality of the school, the management of the school and the medium of instruction did show influence on the level of creative thinking of secondary school students. The boys, urban students, private school students and English medium school students are holding higher level of creative thinking that their counterparts, though all of them hold a high level of creative thinking. The secondary school students should enhance their creative thinking capacity through useful strategies and practices.

The study would be of great use to the administrators, teachers and parents in enhancing the creative thinking capacities of students, the blossoming buds of the growing society.

Dr. Digumarti Bhaskara Rao

Sri Sai Soudha
D-43, S.V.N. Colony
Guntur 522006
A.P., India

CONTENTS

1
INTRODUCTION

INTRODUCTION

Creative thinking is a thinking that produces new methods, new concepts, new understandings, new inventions and new works of art. It is at the very root of human progress. The history of civilisation is the history of man's creative triumphs, from his discovery of fire to his investigations of outer space.

Creativity consists largely of re-arranging what we know in order to find out what we do not know, as opined by George Kneller.

The word "Creativity" is derived from the Latin word "Creatus", which means "to make into observance" (to make into practice), i.e., to bring out the inherent creativity of a person into light and put into practice (which can be turned into real practice (use) of inherent creativity of a person.

Creativity is essentially a human phenomenon and it is a process of systematic thinking. If we think in a systematic manner, we will have a variety of solutions to each problem. Creative people never fear about the problems. They are always busy in finding out the solutions for the problems. They never agree the word "problem". It is very simple to them and they believe that a wide variety of possibilities are available through divergent ideas for any problem. If these possibilities are applied one by one, gradually it leads to the solution of the problem.

All creative are capable, but all capable are not creative. Every one of us has creative potentialities. But we have to work hard to be creative and analyse the problems. As it was done in the past, we are enjoying so many facilities today. If the same could be practiced by all educationalists and teachers; they could not only improve themselves, but also the children of their own and their schools. Parents need to play a vital role in developing creativity in their children, by inspiring them, for future development.

Eminent psychologists like Young, Rogers, MacKinnon, Rolla May, Mednick, Mooney, Murphy, Taylor conducted many experiments on creativity. The essence of creativity, found through their theories, is mainly consisting of five stages, namely, Necessity, Evolution, Synthesis, Application and Different directions. These psychologists emphasised that every one of us could learn these qualities.

J.P. Guilford (1950) stated that "The teaching methods of present educational system are satisfactory, but the boys and girls are of lack of creative thinking. The study without creativity is a blind one." Immediate after this announcement, American educationists inculcated the creativity as a subject in their academic curriculum. This made them to produce marvelous things today and they are now one step ahead of great Russians in all aspects.

The importance of the creative thinking in the modern society increased due to technological revolution. All the progressive nations are trying to develop creative thinking abilities in the new generations. The concept of creative thinking, therefore, occupies a predominant place in pedagogy and educational psychology. Every one is in search of new creations. As the school is considered to be a miniature society, the creative thinking abilities should be cultivated in the minds of the students. Today students are the future citizens who can take the world ahead by discoveries and inventions in the fields of science, literature, teaching, business, art and other fields of human accomplishments. They are responsible for putting up novel ideas and bring about social and cultural changes in the society. It is evident that the progress of a society depends on the development of creative thinking abilities among the people. Hence, it is necessary to develop creativity/creative thinking among the pupils at primary school level itself.

The human nature itself is to be curious about new things and fascinated by novel things. The creative people out of their creative thinking create the novelty. Thinking, at some time and somewhere, may stop but creativity will not stop. It is an endless process. Creativity comes out whenever opportunity arises. It is evident in science exhibitions, science fairs, drawings, essay writing and elocution competitions. Hence, such opportunities that elevate the creative thinking should be inculcated in the minds of children from their school age. If the minds of children are cultivated with creativity from the childhood, there will be a creative world in the future. As the seeds are considered to be the future plants, by sowing creativity in our school curriculum, we too can create more wonders through children.

History of Creativity

In India, Chanukya described the creativity a long ago. So many creative personalities were born in our India from Adi Shankara to Abdul Kalam. Our Indians were the first who introduced the game "chess", the creative play of all games.

The way in which different societies have formulated the concept of creativity has changed throughout history, as has the term "creativity" itself.

The ancient Greeks, who believed that the muses were the source of all inspiration, actually had no terms corresponding "to create" or "creator". The expression "poiein" (to make) sufficed. The sole exception was poetry, the poet was seen as making new things—bringing to life a new world—while the artist merely imitated.

In Rome, this Greek view was modified, and Horace wrote that not only poets but also painters were entitled to the privilege of daring whatever they wished. Unlike Greek, Latin had a term for "creating" (*creatio*) and for "creator", and had two expressions for "to make" — "*facere*" and "create".

Although neither the Greeks nor the Romans had any words that directly corresponded to the word creativity, their art, architecture, music, inventions and discoveries provide numerous examples of what we would today describe as creative works. At the time, the concept of genius probably came closest to describing the creative talents bringing forth these works.

A fundamental change came in the Christian period; "*creatio*" came to designate God's act of "creation from nothing". "*Creatio*", thus, took on a different meaning than "*facere*" (to make), and ceased to apply to human functions. The ancient view that art is not a domain of creativity persisted in that period.

Another shift occurred in more modern times. Renaissance had a sense of their own independence, freedom and creativity, and sought to give voice to this sense of independence and creativity. Baltasar Gracian (1601-1658) wrote, "Art is the completion of nature, as it was a second Creator".

By 18th century and the Age of Enlightenment, the concept of creativity was appearing more often in art theory, and was linked up with the concept of imagination. The Western view of creativity can be contrasted with the Eastern view. For the Hindus, Confucius, Taoists and Buddhists, creation was at most a kind of discovery or mimicry, and the idea of creation from "nothing" had no place in these philosophies and religions.

In 19th century, not only was art regarded as creativity, but also it alone was so regarded. When later, at the turn of 20th century, there began to be discussion of creativity in the sciences (Jan Lukasiewicz, 1878-1956) and in nature (Henri Bergson) this was generally taken as the transference to the sciences of concepts proper to art.

In the late nineteenth and early twentieth centuries, leading mathematicians and scientists such as Hermann von Helmholtz (1896) and Henri Poincare (1908) had begun to reflect on and publicly discuss their creative processes, and these insights were built on in early accounts of the creative process by pioneering theorists such as Graham Wallas (1926) and Max Wertheimer (1945).

However, the formal starting point for the scientific study of creativity, from the standpoint of orthodox psychological literature, is generally considered to have been J. P. Guilford's 1950 address to the American Psychological Association, which helped popularise the topic and focus on a scientific approach to conceptualising creativity and measuring it by means such as psychometric testing. In parallel with these developments, others have taken a more pragmatic approach teaching practical creativity techniques. Three of the best-known among them are Alex Osborn's "brainstorming" (1950s to present), Genrikh Altshuller's Theory of Inventive Problem Solving (TRIZ, 1950s to present), and Edward de Bono's "lateral thinking" (1960s to present).

Creativity is a multidisciplinary and multifaceted concept that held the interest of both theorists and practitioners over many a year. Creativity is perhaps more important today than ever before (Runco, 2004) because of the fast and complex changes that characterise the environment in which we live, operate and adjust or modify.

Meaning of Creativity and Creative Thinking

The following definitions of creativity will help in the understanding its meaning.

According to the Dictionary of Psychology, creative thinking means the achievement of new relationship among the parts of experience.

Creativity is a combination of many abilities running through many spheres of human activity. It is manifested in a variety of ways though essentially it is the process of bringing something new into birth (May, 1953).

An omnibus identification, that was presented by Newell and others (1962), states that thinking may be called creative if: (1) the product has novelty and value either for the thinker or the culture; (2) the thinking is unconventional; (3) it is highly motivated and persistent or of great intensity; and (4) the problem was initially vague and undefined so that part of the task was to formulate the problem itself.

Creativity in education is the 'emergence of new concepts' and views it as the end product of spatiotemporal process (De Roc-Adrian, 1974). Three conditions that are required for it are: (a) originality of response; (b) adaptability; and (c) elaboration.

Jha (1978) defined creativity as the manifestation of uncommon talent in terms of novel and original products (whether ideas or effects) commanding high professional estimate of their worth.

Arnold (1963) says that creativity involves the rearrangements of past experiences with possibly some changes in to new patterns to satisfy some experienced or implied need.

Mednick (1964) says that creative thinking consists of forming new combinations of associative elements which combinations either meet specified requirements or are in some way useful. The more mutually remote the element of the new combination, the more creative is the process or solution.

Guilford defined that creativity sometimes refers to creative potential, sometimes to creative production, and sometimes to creative productivity. Here, creative potential means the personal disposition of the individual in which there are some more or less permanent qualities which help him in creative thinking. Creative thinking leads to new ideas. Creative production does not mean production of concrete things. It means the process of productive thinking. This definition of creativity establishes creative thinking as its primary characteristic. Emphasising this element in creativity, Mednick writes, "Creative thinking consists of forming new combination of associate elements." The most important characteristic of creative thinking is the fact that in it one finds new types of associations in place of their more common varieties.

Guilford (1967) has distinguished three kinds of productive thinking: Deductive thinking, in which an inference or conclusion is deduced logically from information on hand; Inductive thinking, in which the individual goes beyond the present information, adding new elements that are not inherent in the known fact; and evaluative thinking, in which the individual judges the suitability or appropriateness of an idea. All these three may be used in creative thinking. Deductive thinking is creative when the individual sees new relationships that he has not noticed before. Most often, however, creativity requires inductive and evaluative thinking. The individual supplies new formulations or new hypotheses and imagines the possible consequences of untried solutions. Then, as he critically evaluates his work, he may make revisions and changes before it is shaped into final and usable form.

Torrance defined creative thinking as "the process of sensing gaps or disturbing or missing elements, forming ideas or hypotheses, and communicating the results, possibly modifying and retesting the hypotheses". According to this definition of creativity, it is clear that it involves new hypotheses, their testing and constant modification. Further clarifying the process of creative thinking, first of all it is felt, and then the problem is defined and clarified. After this, there is a period of preparation, which involves reading, writing, discussion and research, and gathering possible solutions of the problems. After this, the pros and cons of different solutions are evaluated. In the end of this process, some new idea emerges in the form of insight. This new solution is now examined and new researches are conducted on its basis, which leads to the creation of new principles, methods, pictures, poems, etc.

Sir Fredric described creativity as bold thinking. Bold thinking means divergent thinking, breaking of old norms, having new experiences and creating new combinations.

Simpson emphasised that creative thinking involves new forms of thinking away from the traditional forms. Thus creativity includes curiosity, imagination, research, novelty, inventions, etc.

According to Gestalt theory of creative thinking, creativity involves change of central point, change of meaning and novel organisation. It involves insight, which is the cause of sudden emergence of new ideas. Existentialists have presented a theory similar to the Gestalt theory.

Skinner defined creative thinking that "The predictions and inferences for the individual are new, original, ingenious and unusual. The creative thinker is one who explores new areas and makes new observations, new predictions and new inferences."

The creative thinker is one who explores new areas and makes new observation, new predictions and new inferences. (Gray, 1954)

Therefore, we can conclude that creativity is the capacity or ability of an individual to create, discover or produce a new idea or object including the rearrangement or reshaping of what is already known to him.

We should not be deceived by seeming the simplicity of this procedure. It is simple enough to be effective but it certainly is not automatic. In fact, the creation of new ideas will require tremendous mental effort. Perhaps that is why it is often said that creativity is "painful". Thomas Alva Edison, once, commented that creativity is 90 per cent perspiration and 10 per cent inspiration.

Creativity is...

- Looking at the ordinary and seeing what others don't see
- Passion—being own voice
- Responding to conflict
- Coming out from under
- Inspiration
- Energy
- Perseverance
- Universal
- Sharing
- Spontaneous
- Intuitive
- Own way of interpreting of things around us
- Coming with own ideas
- Drawing, dancing, walking, singing
- Unique, genuine, given easily, capable, reliable
- Freedom to think of new ideas and ways of doing things

- Sense of bringing to well-being
- New interest, focus, happiness, fulfillment
- Thinking out of the box
- Ideas practically formulated into reality
- Imagination acting on life
- Spiritual – from God
- Co-creator with the divine
- Being able to visualise
- Bring unrelated resources together to make something new
- Making something from nothing
- Tapping into the great unconscious

According to a dictionary, creative thinking is a mental process involving the generation of new ideas or concepts, or new associations between existing ideas or concepts. From a scientific point of view, the products of creative thought are usually considered to have both originality and appropriateness. An alternative, more everyday conception of creativity is that it is simply an act of making something new. Although intuitively a simple phenomenon, it is in fact quite complex. It has been studied from the perspectives of behavioural psychology, social psychology, psychometrics, cognitive science, artificial intelligence, philosophy, history, economics, design research, business, and management among others. The studies have covered everyday creativity, exceptional creativity and even artificial creativity. Unlike many phenomena in science, there is no single authoritative perspective or definition of creativity. Creativity has been attributed variously to define intervention, cognitive process, the social environment, personal traits, and chance ('accident', 'serendipity'). It has been associated with genius, mental illness and humour. Some say it is a trait we are born with; others say it can be taught with the application of simple techniques.

Characteristic Elements of Creativity

The following are the specific characteristic elements of creativity:

- Creativity is a process not a product.
- The process is goal-directed, either for personal benefit or for the benefit of the social group.
- It leads to the production of something new, different, and therefore, unique for the person whether it is verbal or non-verbal, concrete or abstract.
- Creativity comes from divergent thinking, while conformity and everyday problem solving comes from convergent thinking.
- The ability to create depends on the acquisition of accepted knowledge.
- Creativity is a form of controlled imagination that leads to some kind of achievement, whether in painting, block building or day-dreaming.

Conditions for Creative Thinking

Creativity involves creative thinking; its characters are factuality, novelty, freedom and harmony. Creative thinking requires several conditions.

- First of all, there should be the capacity to grasp new ideas.
- Secondly, there should be ability of involvement with the object. The creative persons can stay involved in their work for weeks, months and years tirelessly.
- Thirdly, the creative persons should be able to understand the questions involved in the given problem, since only then they can arrive at the solution.
- Fourthly, the creative persons should learn from past failures and reform their thinking.
- Fifthly, the creative persons should have the capacity of detachment from the environment.

Enhancement of Creative Thinking

Factors that enhance creative thinking in individuals or organisations may be divided into two categories, viz., personal and environmental. Personal characteristics that enhance creative ability include high evaluation of aesthetic qualities, having broad interests, curiosity and a penchant for discovery, openness to suggestion, and attraction to complexity, having independence of judgment, thought and action, a love for autonomy, intuition, self-confidence, ability to accommodate ambiguity and to resolve antinomies, intrinsic motivation and a firm belief in self as a creative person.

Environmental factors examine the context in which creative thinking ability is nurtured and in which creative action is required. In an individuals formative stages, family background and structure (Sulloway, 1996), societal norms and values, social institutions such as schools, religion, role models, peer groups, etc., will play a role in the nurturing of creative thinking ability. Contexts that are flexible about rules and regulations, permitting experimentation and independent choices will enhance creativity. Those that are rigid will inhibit it. In the organisational context, situations that avail time to think, resources to spend, encouragement and reward for original solutions, freedom from criticism and that have good role models and norms in which innovation is prized and failure is not fatal, will enhance creative thinking.

Conditions that Foster Creative Thinking

1. *Time:* To be creative, children must not be so regimented that they have little free time to toy with ideas and concepts and try them out in new and original forms.

2. *Solitude:* Only when away from the pressures imposed on them by the social group then only children can be creative. As Singer explained, "it takes time and solitude to develop a rich imaginative life".

3. *Encouragement:* Regardless of how far short of adult standards their achievements fall, children must be encouraged to be creative and free from the ridicule and criticism that far too often are heaped on creative children.

4. *Materials:* Play materials and later other materials must be supplied to stimulate experimentation and exploration that are essential elements of all creativity.
5. *Stimulating Environment:* Both home and school environments must stimulate creativity by providing guidance and encouragement to use the materials that will encourage creativity. This should be done as early as possible from babyhood stage continued through the school years by making creativity an enjoyable and socially recognised experience.
6. *Impassive Parent-Child Relationship:* Parents who are neither over-protective nor over-possessive encourage their children to be independent and self-reliant, two qualities that contribute heavily to creative thinking.
7. *Child-Training Methods:* Democratic and permissive child training in the home and school foster while authoritarian training stifles it.
8. *Opportunities to acquire Knowledge:* Creative thinking cannot take place in vacuum. The more knowledge children can acquire, the better the foundations on which to build creative productions. As Pulaski has said, "children must have content in order to fantasise".

Critical Periods in Development of Creative Thinking

A. *5 to 6 years of age:* Children are ready to enter school at this age. They learn to accept authority and conform to the rules and regulations of adults in the home and later they face the some authority in the school. So they stifle in creative thinking.

B. *8 to 10 years of age:* The desire to be accepted as a member of a gang reaches its peak at this time. Most of the children feel to be accepted. But they must conform as closely as possible to the pattern set by the gang and any deviation is a threat to acceptance.

C. *13 to 15 years of age:* Striving for peer approval especially from members of opposite sex controls the young adolescent pattern of behaviour. Like the gang-age child, the young adolescent conforms in the hope of winning approval and acceptance.

D. *17 to 19 years of age:* At this age striving for approval and acceptance as well as training for a chosen vocation may curb creativity. If the vocation necessitates conforming to a standard pattern and following specific orders and rules, as in most routine jobs, it will stifle creative thinking.

Values of Creative Thinking

Popular about the value of creative thinking centers on what the creative person produces for the benefit and enjoyment of the social group and for social progress. The value of creativity to the person who is creative has often been almost completely overlooked. These values are much too important to be overlooked, as the following facts will attest to.

Creative thinking gives children tremendous personal pleasure and satisfaction—rewards that have a marked influence on their developing personalities. Nothing, for example, give young children more satisfaction than to create something all by themselves, whether it be a house made out of a tuned-over chair covered by a blanket or a drawing of a pet dog. And nothing is more ego-deflating than to have the creation criticised or ridiculed or to be asked what it is supposed to be.

Being creative is also valuable to young children because it adds spice to their play—the activities around which their life centers. If creative thinking can make play pleasurable, children will be happy and contented. This in turn, will lead to good personal and social adjustments.

As children grow older, achievement is of major importance in their adjustment to life. Creative thinking that helps them to achieve success in areas that matter to them and are favourably viewed by people who are significant to them will be a source of great ego satisfaction.

One very important value of creative thinking is that often overlooked is its contribution to leadership. At any age, the leader must contribute something to group that is important to the group members. The child leaders contribution may be in the form of suggestions for a new and different kinds of play activity, or it may be suggestions about how to organise the gang into committees, each with special roles and special responsibilities to the group. In addition to the personal satisfaction children derive from creative thinking, they add to it the satisfaction of playing a leadership role, which will guarantee good social as well as personal adjustments.

The value of creative thinking is highlighted in the case of children who lack creativity. As Spock has commented, "the person who is strictly literal-minded has a limited usefulness to the world and a limited capacity for joy".

Just because creative thinking is valuable does not mean that the more creative people are the greater will be their contributions to the social group and happier and better adjusted they will be. Too much creative thinking is very likely to make people into impractical dreamers'—those who create mentally but never seem to be able to put their dreams into practical forms that will benefit them or the social group. As a result, they will not achieve what they are potentially capable. This will result in feelings of failure, which are damaging to personal as well as social adjustments.

Discovery of Creative Thinking

In the past, creative people were discovered only after they had produced something original, such as a picture, a musical composition, or an invention. With our present knowledge of what ability to be creative, commonly known as talent, can be fostered or stifled by environmental influences. It has become apparent that waiting until the creative person has produced something worthy of attention may, for most children, mean waiting until it is too late.

Consequently, interest today is centered on ways of discovering potential creative thinking so that it can be given an opportunity to develop. Discovering potential creative thinking has proved to be a very difficult task. In the search, effort has been directed toward the construction of tests that will measure creative thinking or some aspect of it.

Teachers try to identify creative thinking by determining how original children are in solving problems or how much of a 'personal touch' they give to story telling, art work or compositions. These judgments are of necessity, subjective and consequently, of little scientific value. For the teacher, however, they serve as guidelines in discovering and encouraging creative thinking. For parents and others whose work is related to guiding the child's development, similar approaches must be used. Until reliable objective tests can be developed, creative thinking must have necessarily been discovered by the way it is expressed in the child's activities.

Creativity Quotient

Several attempts have been made to develop a Creativity Quotient of an individual similar to the Intelligence Quotient (IQ), however these efforts have been unsuccessful. Most measures of creativity are dependent on the personal judgment of the tester, so a standardised measure is difficult to develop.

Psychometric Approach of Creative Thinking

The group of J.P. Guilford, which pioneered the modern psychometric study of creativity, constructed several tests to measure creativity in 1967 that include: *Plot Titles*, where participants are given the plot of a story and asked to write original titles; *Quick Responses* is a word-association test scored for uncommonness; *Figure Concepts*, where participants were given simple drawings of objects and individuals are asked to find out qualities or features that are common by two or more drawings, these were scored for uncommonness; *Unusual Uses* is finding unusual uses for everyday common objects such as bricks; *Remote Associations*, where participants are asked to find a word between two given words (e.g., Hand _____ Call); and *Remote Consequences*, where participants are asked to generate a list of consequences of unexpected events (e.g. loss of gravity).

Based on Guilford's work, Torrance developed the 'Torrance Tests of Creative Thinking' in 1974. They involved simple tests of divergent thinking and other problem-solving skills, which were scored on: *Fluency*: The total number of interpretable, meaningful, and relevant ideas generated in response to the stimulus; *Flexibility*:

The number of different categories of relevant responses; *Originality*: The statistical rarity of the responses among the test subjects; and *Elaboration*: The amount of detail in the responses.

The Creativity Achievement Questionnaire, a self-report test that measures creative achievement across 10 domains, was described in 2005 and shown to be reliable and valid when compared to other measures of creativity and to independent evaluation of creative output.

Social-Personality Approach of Creative Thinking

Some researchers have taken a 'social-personality approach' to the measurement of creativity. In these studies, personality traits such as independence of judgment, self-confidence, attraction to complexity, aesthetic orientation and risk-taking are used as measures of the creativity of individuals. Other researchers have related creativity to the trait, openness to experience.

Genrich Altshuller in the 1950s introduced approaching creativity as an exact science with TRIZ and a Level-of-Invention measure.

Creativity in Various Contexts

Creativity has been studied from a variety of perspectives and is important in numerous contexts. Most of these approaches are unidisciplinary and it is, therefore, difficult to form a coherent overall view. The following sections examine some of the areas in which creativity is seen as being important.

Creativity in Diverse Cultures

Creativity is a scientific concept, which is mostly rooted within a Western creationist perspective. Francois Jullien in 'Process and Creation' (1989) is invited to look at that concept from a Chinese cultural point of view.

Todd Lubart has studied extensively the cultural aspects of creativity and innovation.

Rody Roderick Klein together with Metis Reflective Community have also published a few papers on Metis, a sort of cosmogonic approach to creativity rooted on a concept of universe where everything is both a constraint and/or an opportunity and interconnected. A universe, without totality, is a continuous creative process. Metis bares its name from the work of Destiennes and Vernant on our Greek heritage displaying a special outlook on wisdom, creativity and intelligence. It is a constant holistic creation process and the human self perception of his contribution to this process could be enhanced by a trace composer.

Pierre Levy has created the Information Economy Meta Language (ieml). This computable language could be used in order to reach an interdisciplinary view of creativity, innovation and intelligence.

Creativity in Art and Literature

Most people associate creativity with the fields of art and literature. In these fields, originality is considered to be a sufficient condition for creativity unlike other fields where both originality and appropriateness are necessary. Within the different modes of artistic expression, one can postulate a continuum extending from 'interpretation' to 'innovation'. Established artistic movements and genres pull practitioners to the 'interpretation' end of the scale, whereas original thinkers strive towards the 'innovation' pole. Not that we conventionally expect some creative people (dancers, actors, orchestral members, etc.) to perform (interpret) while allowing others (writers, painters, composers, etc.) more freedom to express the new and the different.

Creative Industries and Services

Today, creativity forms the core activity of a growing section of the global economy — the so-called "creative industries" — capitalistically generating (generally non-tangible) wealth through the creation and exploitation of intellectual property or through the provision of creative services. The creative professional workforce is becoming a more integral part of industrialised nations' economies.

Creative professions include writing, art, design, theater, television, radio, motion pictures, related crafts, computing, as well as marketing strategy, some aspects of scientific research and development, product development, some types of teaching and curriculum design, and more. Since many creative professionals (actors and writers, for example) are also employed in secondary professions.

Creativity is also seen as being increasingly important in a variety of other professions. Architecture and industrial design are the fields most often associated with creativity, and more generally the fields of design and design research. These fields explicitly value creativity and journals such as 'Design Studies' have published many studies on creativity and creative problem solving. Fields such as science and engineering have, by contrast, experienced a less explicit (but arguably no less important) relation to creativity. Simonton shows how some of the major scientific advances of the 20th century can be attributed to the creativity of individuals. This ability will also be seen as increasingly important for engineers in years to come.

Accounting has also been associated with creativity with the popular euphemism creative accounting. Although this term often implies unethical practices, Amabile has suggested that even this profession can benefit from the (ethical) application of creative thinking.

Critical issue related to creativity is the problem of identifying the potential and various types of criteria to assets.

Getzels and Madovs (1969) summarised them under the following categories:

(i) *Achievement:* Highly recognised achievements like a noble prize or any other mark of outstanding accomplishment as an index of creativity (Ghiselish, 1952);

(ii) *Rating:* Evaluation by peers, teachers, supervisors, experts, etc. (Mackinon, 1964, Drevdahl, 1964);

(iii) *Intelligence:* Performance by intelligence test, superior I.Q. as a criterion (Terman, 1925);

(iv) *Personality:* Evaluation of personality characterisations in relation to appropriate profile of creative personality (Cattell and Drevadh, 1955);

(v) *Creativity test scores:* Performance on the creative tests such as those developed by Flanagan (1958), Buhl (1960), Guilford and Marrifield (Meldrick, 1960), and Medric (1964), Torrance (1966) and others.

Lackler suggested that the creativity of contribution might be measured in terms of the extent of the area of Science, which it covers.

The Committee appointed by Utah Conference (1959) recommended that the first object of study, when such products are judged to be "creative", the behaviour which produced measure should provide degrees which produced them can be called creative. The criterion measure should provide degree or levels of possession of the trait, using the most basic and unequivocal measures available. The committee includes the following as proofs of creative products: new theories, hypotheses, classificatory or analytical concepts, relationships, formulas, techniques, materials and physical or temporal patterns. They differentiate these from discoveries of things or events which pre-existed recognising that such discoveries might involve a creative act.

Utah Conference (Taylor, 1959) presented about the line of the variables and dimensions, potentially involved criteria of creativity. The committee recommended that the identification of the productive processes involved in divergent and convergent thinking and of work methods such as flexibility, planning, perseverance and a variety of approaches.

Measurement of Creative Thinking

There are so many tests available for measuring the creativity of children. The mentionable are Minnesota Test of Creative Thinking, Torrance Test of Thinking, Remote Association Test, Wallach and Kogan's Creativity Instruments, Baquer Mehdi's Tests of Creative Thinking.

The creative aspect in the child can also be assessed through some non-testing devices like Natural Observation Method, Situational Techniques, Rating Scale, Check List, Interview, Personality Inventories, Interest Inventories, Attitude Scales, Aptitude Tests, Value Schedules, and Projective Techniques, etc.

Some of the major efforts in the measurement of creativity may be summarised briefly.

Coulin (1902) made more use of his measures based on compositions with high school students than with younger groups. Asramson (1927) used inkblots and concrete observations with high school students as well as with grades three through six. Harmes (1939) applied his test in which subjects drew lines to represent words (mostly action words). M.D. Vernon (1948) used his imaginative construction test (stories based as four coloured pictures) with high school subjects, as did Stephenson (1949) with his poetry-writing task. Most of recent work with high school students has involved adoptions of Guilford's test with few innovations. Gerzels and Jackson (1958) used four adapted talks (words associations, uses of things, hidden shapes, the tables) and construction one of own make up problems. With seventh grade subjects, McGuire, Hindsman and Jennings (1961) used the zeal ford tests, viz., rhymes, unusual uses, consequences, common situations, seeking problems, mutilated words and gestalt completion. Denieh and Quacken Bush (1960) administrated the measures to seventh and eighth graders, viz., consequences, plots tiles and unusual uses. Guilford (1961) gave a process report on his work which he has administrated his battery to ninth graders and found essentially the same factors he found with adults.

Creative growth has rarely been recognised as an objective of secondary education. Although many promising changes in objectives seem to be occurring especially in high school subjects like mathematics, physics and chemistry, the results of a 1959-60 sample survey (Torrance, 1960) of Minnesota social teachers probably reflects the status of high school objective in this regard. The references were as follows: Cognitive - 70.7%, Memory - 5.3%, Convergent - 18.7%, Divergent - 1.7% and Evaluation - 3.6%

Guilford's Tests, emerged from his factor analysis studies (Guilford and Merrifield, 1960) and Torrance Test of Creative Thinking (Torrance, 1966) are most prominent among them and are widely used by hundreds of investigators. Some other prominent tests of creativity are the Wallach and Kogan instruments for creativity, the Getzel and Jackson test of creative thinking, Battery of originality tests by Barron, Flanagan remote association tests and Minnesota tests of creative thinking.

A good number of tests of creativity have been developed in India during seventies (Passi, 1972; Maul, 1973; Majumdar, 1973; Chauhan and Tiwari, 1974; Ramachandra char, 1975; and Kundely, 1977). Some other prominent tests are Kerala University test of creative thinking and tests of scientific creativity of Grewal and Singh. Most of these tests are based on Guilford's of creative thinking or on the lines of Torrance's test model. Many of them measure general creativity but some are developed to measure creativity in specific area of content. For example, Majumdar (1973) has developed the creativity test battery to measure scientific creativity for the scientific talent search scheme of National Council of Education Research and Training, whereas Kundley (1979) developed his creativity in Marathi. Most of the creativity tests in India are developed for the doctoral studies. Some of them are published and now many are commercially available.

Inhibitors of Creative Thinking

Among the factors that inhibit creative thinking ability in individuals and organisations are a population that is not curious or inquisitive and unwilling or unable to question assumptions, resistance to change and tendency to conform, fear of failure and criticism, red tape, time pressure (time is important for new ideas to incubate), lack of feedback, inappropriate norms and values, strict adherence to rules, regulations and budgets, an atmosphere characterised by constraint and lack of autonomy, blinked thinking and unrealistic expectations, over analysis of phenomenon (resulting in paralysis), organisational structures that constrain the flow of ideas, lack of recognition and reward for successful ideas, short term orientation and departmental actions that fail to take into account the bigger picture (functional myopia).

There are also a number of factors that may work both ways—that may stimulate or inhibit creative thinking. Among these are: lack of resources – ideas require extensive resources to be developed but paucity may in itself be an incentive for creativity (Runco, 2004);

competition may also act in both directions – it may stimulate creative thinking to maintain a competitive edge but it may also discourage creative thinking effort by making obsolete innovations before they are able to recoup expenditure on their development.

Hazards to Creativity

Creativity is so important to good personal and social adjustments that anything that prevents its development is hazardous. When environment conditions foster the development of mental rigidity or convergent thinking, it will prevent the development of mental flexibility or divergent thinking.

Equally serious is anything that encourages spending too much time on certain forms of creativity that it engaged in occasionally, may bring favourable results but not if engaged in excessively. Occasional daydreaming, for example, may lead to good personal and social adjustments, but excessive daydreaming not only counteracts the good effects of daydreaming but it also proves to be harmful to these adjustments.

There are a number of hazards to good adjustments in different areas of creativity. A survey of these hazards will highlight potential hazards in this area of the child's development and explain why and under what conditions they are hazardous.

Failures to Stimulate Creativity

Even though the foundations for creativity are innate like all innate potentials; its development must be stimulated. Any condition that obstructs this stimulation will prevent its development.

Evidence, as was pointed out earlier, indicates that creativity appears early and is first shown in the way a baby play with toys. At this time, any condition that obstructs its development may stifle it. One of the most common obstacles is lack of stimulation.

Lack of stimulation may come from ignorance of its importance on the part of parents and other people in the baby's environment, or it may come from the assumption that because creativity is an inborn characteristic, nature will provide for its development and stimulation is, therefore unnecessary.

When children are old enough to go to school whether nursery school, kindergarten, or first grade, they may be given stimulation but, by then, it may be too late. By that time, they may have become so accustomed to following a pattern set by others or to thinking in the way others think. No amount of stimulation, then, will be adequate to break completely the habits already formed.

Inability to Detect Creativity in Time

Until young have knowledge and skills on which to build creative thinking and activities, there will be no sure way for people in their environments to know what their potentials for creativity are. And, until there are tests to detect potential creativity, they will have no way to spot these potentials.

Under such conditions, it is not surprising that stimulation to the development of creativity is neglected. By the time there is some evidence that the child has the potential for creativity, it may be too late for stimulation to result in the full development of these potentials.

Until tests or other methods can be devised to spot creativity at an early age, the only way to overcome this hazard is to go on the assumption that every child has the potential for creativity, though, in varying degrees and to provide the necessary stimulation at an early age. If this is done, many potentially creative children will be given an opportunity to develop their creativity.

Unfavourable Social Attitudes Towards Creativity

Social factors often agitate against the development of creativity. These obstructive factors take to common forms: first, unfavourable attitude toward children who are creative and second, lack of social reward for creativity.

Children soon discover that creativity is less of an asset than a high IQ in meeting the demands of the school. They also discover that the school encourages and rewards convergent or conventional thinking more than potentially creative divergent thinking.

Not only do obstructive social and lack of rewards discourage creativity, but even worse, they often foster maladjustive behaviour by developing in the child an unfavourable self-concept. While some creative children may withdraw from a social group that has a poor opinion of them, others are likely to retaliate by being troublesome and vindictive.

Unfavourable Home Conditions

Within the home, there are many conditions that affect the development of creativity. Because the home is the child's first environment, any condition that stifles the development of creativity when it is maturational ready to develop can be most damaging. Furthermore, conditions that stifle the development of creativity when the child is young are likely to persist and stifle the development of creativity, as the child grows older.

Of the many possible home conditions that are unfavourable to the development of creativity, the most common are discouragement of exploration, regimentation of time, encouragement of family togetherness, discouragement of fantasy, and provision of highly structured play equipment, conservative parents, overprotective parents and authoritarian discipline.

Unfavourable School Conditions

School conditions also affect the development of creativity. If they are unfavourable, they can counteract much of the stimulation of creativity provided by a favourable home environment. This is one of the reasons why the age of school entry is a 'critical period' in the development of creativity.

Among many school conditions that discourage the development of creativity are very large classes where regimentation is essential, strong emphasis on memorising; discouragement of anything that does not fall within the prescribed pattern, whether it be original paining or original storytelling; highly organised schedule of class activities; strict, authoritarian discipline; and the belief of teachers that creative children are hard to manage and their work harder to grade than that of the conformers. If teachers regard academic achievement as the only path to success in life, the obstacles to creative expression may be over-whelming.

Contributions of Creative Thinking in Psychology and Cognitive Science

The study of mental representations and processes underlying creative thinking belongs to the domains of psychology and cognitive science.

A psychodynamic approach to understanding creative thinking was proposed by Sigmund Freud, who suggested that creativity arises as a result of frustrated desires for fame, fortune, and love, with the energy that was previously tied up in frustration and emotional tension in the neurosis being sublimated into creative thinking activity. But, Freud later retracted this view later.

Graham Wallas (1926) presented one of the first models of the creative thinking process. In the Wallas Stage Model, creative insights and illuminations may be explained by a process consisting of 5 stages:

(i) ***Preparation*** (preparatory work on a problem that focuses the individual's mind on the problem and explores the problem's dimensions);

(ii) Incubation (where the problem is internalised into the unconscious mind and nothing appears externally to be happening);

(iii) ***Intimation*** (the creative person gets a feeling that a solution is on its way);

(iv) ***Illumination*** or *insight* (where the creative idea bursts forth from its preconscious processing into conscious awareness); and

(v) ***Verification*** (where the idea is consciously verified, elaborated, and then applied).

In numerous publications, Wallas' model is just treated as four stages, with 'intimation' seen as a sub-stage. There has been some empirical research looking at whether, as the concept of 'incubation' in Wallas' model implies, a period of interruption or rest from a problem may aid creative problem-solving. Ward lists various hypotheses that have been advanced to explain why incubation may aid creative problem-solving, and notes how some empirical evidence is consistent with the hypothesis that incubation aids creative problem-solving in that it enables forgetting of misleading clues. Absence of incubation may lead the problem solver to become fixated on inappropriate strategies of solving the problem. This work disputes the earlier hypothesis that creative solutions to problems arise mysteriously from the unconscious mind while the conscious mind is occupied on other tasks. Wallas considered creativity to be a legacy of the evolutionary process, which allowed humans to quickly adapt to rapidly changing environments. Simonton provides an updated perspective on this view in his book, Origin of Genius: Darwinian Perspectives on Creative Thinking.

Guilford performed important work in the field of create thinking, drawing a distinction between convergent and divergent production (commonly renamed convergent and divergent thinking). Convergent thinking involves aiming for a single and correct solution to a problem, whereas divergent thinking involves creative generation of multiple answers to a set problem. Divergent thinking is sometimes used as a synonym for creativity in the literature of psychology. Other researchers have occasionally used the terms flexible thinking or fluid intelligence, which are roughly similar to (but not synonymous with) creativity.

Koestler lists three types of creative individuals—the *Artist*, the *Sage* and the *Jester*. Believers in this trinity hold all three elements necessary in business and can identify them all in 'truly creative' companies as well. Koestler introduced the concept of bisociation, in which creative thinking arises as a result of intersection of two quite different frames of reference.

Finke, et al (1992) proposed the Geneplore Model, in which creative thinking takes place in two phases: a generative phase, where an individual constructs mental representations called pre-inventive structures and an exploratory phase where those structures are used to come up with creative ideas. Weisberg argued, by contrast, that creative thinking only involves ordinary cognitive processes yielding extraordinary results.

In 1990s, various approaches in cognitive science that dealt with metaphor, analogy and structure mapping have been converging and a new integrative approach to the study of creative thinking in science, art and humour has emerged under the label Conceptual Blending.

In general sense, all problem solving is creative thinking; each problem is unique in certain respects and each solution requires the integration of ideas into new and meaningful patterns. On another level, creative thinking may manifest itself in the speculations of the philosopher and the hypotheses of the scientist; on still another, in the works of the painter, the sculptor, the composer, the novelist, and the poet. On the everyday level, there is the creative thinking that changes one's own personality. It can produce insights into some phase of oneself or one's world which one has not seen before, insights which may drastically alter one's assumptions, motives, and ways of behaving. In every case and at every level, creativity brings into existence something that is new.

In the history of the world, there have been several philosophers, poets, writers and painters, who were turned out their school classes, called backward students, but in later life they created great works. People like Mohandas K. Gandhi, Lincoln, Newton, Shakespeare, Russell and Leonardo da Vinci were the creative individuals, who imposed their marks in their respective fields. Certainly, they were endowed with creative abilities but the role of environment in terms of education, training and opportunities for it cannot be over-ruled. A good education, proper care and provision of opportunities for creative expression inspire, stimulate and shape the creative mind and herein the parents, society and teachers need to shape and sharpen the creative minds. They are required to help the children in nourishing and utilising their creative thinking abilities to the maximum degree. Therefore, educational process, either formal or informal, should be aimed to develop creative thinking abilities among the children. It needs to acquaint children with the actual meaning, the knowledge of creative thinking and ways and means of developing creativity and creative thinking.

STATEMENT OF THE PROBLEM

A Study of Creative Thinking of Secondary School Students

NEED FOR THE STUDY

Today, creative thinking forms the core activity of a growing section of the global economy — the so-called creative industries — capitalistically generating (generally non-tangible) wealth through the creation and exploitation of intellectual property or through the provision of creative services. The creative professional workforce is becoming a more integral part of the economy of industrialised nations. Creative professions include writing, art, design, theater, television, radio, motion pictures and related crafts, as well as marketing, strategy, some aspects of scientific research and development, product development, some types of teaching and curriculum design, etc. Since many creative professionals (actors and writers, for example) are also employed in secondary professions, estimates of creative professionals are often inaccurate.

Creative thinking is also seen as being increasingly important in a variety of other professions. Architecture and industrial design are the fields most often associated with creativity, and more generally the fields of design and design research. These fields explicitly value creativity. Fields such as science and engineering have, by contrast, experienced a less explicit (but arguably no less important) relation to creativity.

Accounting has also been associated with creativity with the popular euphemism creative accounting. Although this term often implies unethical practices, Amabile has suggested that even this profession can benefit from the (ethical) application of creative thinking. Amabile argued that to enhance creativity in business, three components were needed: Expertise (technical, procedural and intellectual knowledge), Creative thinking skills (how flexibly and imaginatively people approach problems), and Motivation (especially intrinsic motivation).

In the early 20th century, Joseph Schumpeter introduced the Economic Theory of Creative Destruction, to describe the way in which old ways of doing things are endogenously destroyed and replaced by the new.

Creative thinking is also seen by economists such as Paul Roomer as an important element in the recombination of elements to produce new technologies and products and, consequently, economic growth. Creativity leads to capital, and creative products are protected by intellectual property laws. Creativity is also an important aspect in understanding entrepreneurship.

The creative class is seen by some to be an important driver of modern economies. The economist Richard Florida (2002) popularised the notion that regions with 3 Ts (Technology, Talent and Tolerance) of economic development also have high concentrations of creative professionals and tend to have a higher level of economic development.

Daniel Pink (2005) argued that we are entering a new age where creative thinking is becoming increasingly important. In this conceptual age, we will need to foster and encourage right-directed thinking (representing creativity and emotion) over left-directed thinking (representing logical and analytical thought).

Nickerson provides a summary of the various creativity techniques that have been proposed. These include approaches that have been developed by both academia and industry; all the creativity techniques are represented in diagrammatic form as in the given below:

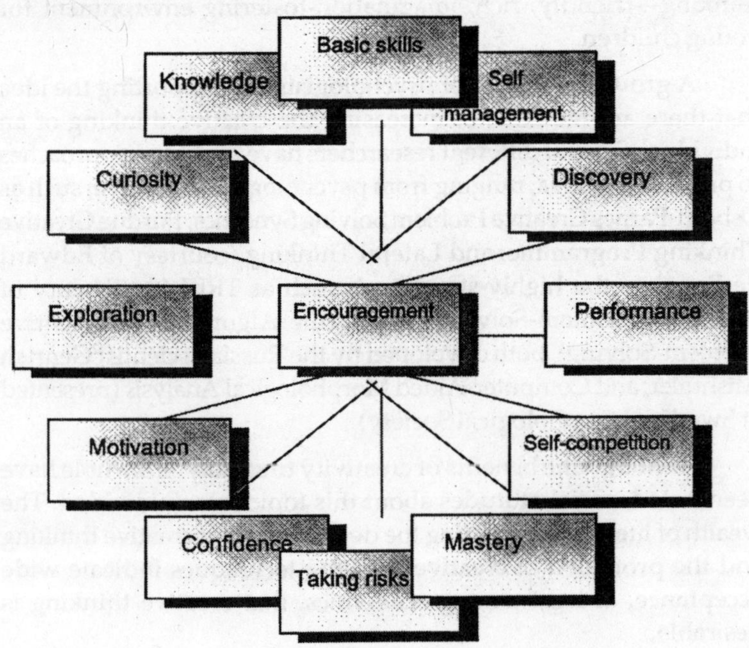

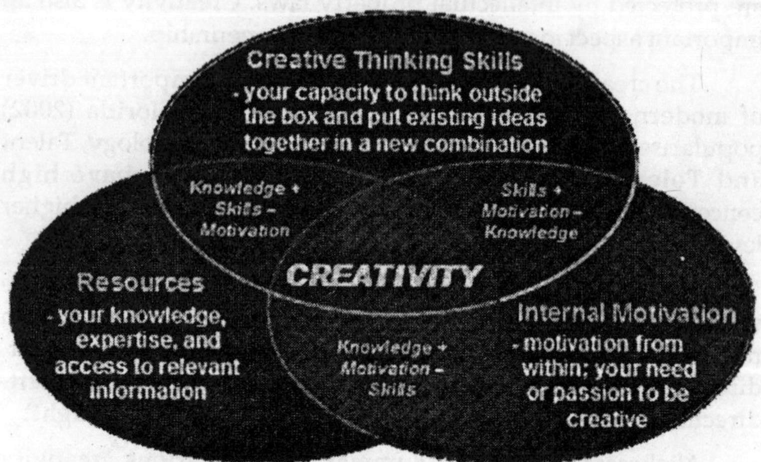

Some see the conventional system of schooling as stifling of creative thinking and attempt (particularly in the pre-school/ kindergarten and early school years) to provide a creative thinking—friendly, rich, imagination-fostering environment for young children.

A growing number of psychologists are supporting the idea that there are methods of increasing the creative thinking of an individual. Several different researchers have proposed approaches to prop up this idea, ranging from psychological-cognitive, such as Osborn-Parnes Creative Problem Solving Synectics; Purdue Creative Thinking Programme; and Lateral Thinking (courtesy of Edward de Bono) to the highly-structured, such as TRIZ (the Theory of Inventive Problem-Solving), ARIZ (the Algorithm of Inventive Problem-Solving), both developed by the Russian scientist Genrich Altshuller; and Computer-Aided Morphological Analysis (presented at Swedish Morphological Society).

Although the benefits of creativity to society as a whole have been noted, social attitudes about this topic remain divided. The wealth of literature regarding the development of creative thinking and the profusion of creative thinking techniques indicate wide acceptance, at least among academics, that creative thinking is desirable.

There is, however, a dark side to creativity, in that it represents a *"quest for a radical autonomy apart from the constraints of social responsibility"*. In other words, by encouraging creative thinking, we are encouraging a departure from society's existing norms and values. Expectation of conformity runs contrary to the spirit of creativity. Nevertheless, employers are increasingly valuing creative thinking skills. A report by the Business Council of Australia, for example, has called for a higher level of creative thinking in graduates. The ability to 'think outside the box' is highly sought after. However, the above-mentioned paradox may well imply that firms pay lip service to thinking outside the box while maintaining traditional, hierarchical organisation structures in which individual creativity is not rewarded.

While creative thinking has been associated with problem solving and value enhancing through proactive actions, it has also been linked with potential costs to the individual and to the society at large. For example, creative geniuses have been associated with various disorders including madness and eccentricity (Ludwig, 1995), alcoholism (Noble, et al, 1993) and stress (Carson and Runco, 1999). Runco (1999) suggested that because creativity is strongly linked to originality it is a kind of social deviance. Plucker and Runco (1999) and Runco (1999) observed that there is frequent stigma attached to creativity. Before these, McLaren (1993) made an observation that it is the dark side of creativity and has given the world weapons of mass destruction and other evil inventions and techniques. It would, of course, be naïve to conclude that creative persons are mad, social deviants or terrorists from such correlations.

It is confirmed that creative thinking exists in many forms and in many individuals. It may be perceived by a teacher or an engineer or a cook or even an ordinary mechanic, who just by listening to engine, senses the problem of a machine. So, a creative person is far more alert, curious and dynamic in thinking; he is flexible, original and novel; he presents new associations, he has divergent thinking; and he has innovative approaches and shows positive thinking. Creativity may be found in the child who may use a peculiar colour combination while painting. A poet may end the poem in a novel way. Thus, creativity can be exhibited in any field such as in architecture, in fashion designing, in interior decoration, in flower arrangement, in salad arrangement or even in deciding the layout of a small house. The only problem is to accept the novel ideas and appreciate them. Otherwise, the usual response to some novel combinations is 'what a mess is this!', which suppresses the creativity at the root itself.

With the above points of discussion, the present study has been undertaken to study the creative thinking of secondary school students.

SCOPE OF THE STUDY

The students studying in ninth class in the secondary schools of Nellore district, Andhra Pradesh are considered for the present study. The variables of the study are boys and girls, rural area versus urban area, government versus private, residential versus non-residential and English medium versus Telugu medium. Thus this study is limited to the variables such as gender, age, locality, management, and medium of instruction.

OBJECTIVES OF THE STUDY

The present study is planned to proceed with the following objectives:

1. To assess the level of creative thinking of secondary school students;
2. To find out the level of creative thinking of secondary school boys and girls;
3. To find out the level of creative thinking of rural and urban secondary school students;
4. To find out the level of creative thinking of Telugu medium and English medium secondary school students;
5. To find out the level of creative thinking of government and private secondary school students.

EDUCATIONAL IMPLICATIONS

Suggestions may be given to enhance the creative thinking of the secondary school students after identifying their level of creative thinking as it helps a student in the following manner:

1. Students will be able to think systematically (divergently);
2. Students can express the ideas as fluently as possible;
3. The capacity to take independent decisions while solving their academic problems can be improved;
4. They can, not only solve the problems but also finds novel solutions to the problems in all walks of life by having good creative power;
5. They can attempt several competitive exams;
6. The private organisations are mainly interested in those who are creative. They select the creative students in the campus interviews while studying in their institutions. The ability of creative thinking helps them to win the interview in an easy way;
7. Creative thinking may have great impact on the intellectual and personality development by exercising the mental faculties;
8. Creative thinking helps a person whatever the field they choose, i.e., management, administration, art, teaching, business, commerce, engineering, architecture, fashion designing, author, poet, dramatist, etc.;
9. Students can possess high aesthetic values and good aesthetic judgment.

2

REVIEW OF RELATED RESEARCH

Review of related literature provides theories, ideas and explanations of a new problem. It suggests methods, procedures, sources of data and statistical techniques appropriate to the solution of the problem. It also helps to sharpen and define understanding of existing knowledge of the problem area and provides a background for the research project.

It helps the researcher in the identification of the problem, in the selection of methods, tools and data analysis techniques and also in guarding against the likely pit falls in the process of research. The researcher stands to gain from the experiences of other early researches in the field and gets guidance from them. He/she collects all possible solutions to the problem under study, all possible ways of interpreting the phenomenon being studied or all possible ways of understanding the true nature of the knowledge being discovered. From all the possibilities so collected, the researcher will select a feasible one to try out.

The search for related literature is a time consuming process. Even then, it is necessary for a good research. Hence, this chapter is meant for the study and citation of the research studies related to the present study.

The first Indian study in the area of correlates of creativity was conducted by Bhattacharya in 1956. Later on, this area could attract the attention of many more Indian researchers. It resulted into a large number of studies at masters and doctorate levels. In these studies, creativity was studied in relation to different variables. These variables have been clustered into three groups. The first group is named as demographic which includes 'age', 'birth order', 'sex', 'locality' and 'socio-economic status' variables. The second group is cognitive and it includes variables like 'academic subjects', 'intelligence' and 'scholastic achievement'. The last group is termed as affective, which includes variables related to 'values' and 'personality'. Samples for these studies were drawn from various levels, such as primary, middle, secondary and college. But majority of studies were conducted with secondary school population. The findings related to each one of these variables in the context of creative thinking (as of creativity) are given separately under different heads.

1. Creative Thinking and Age

Raina (1970) studied the relationship between age and total creativity along with its components. Of these, total creativity, originality, and elaboration were found to be positively and significantly related with age. The relationship between age and fluency was negative and significant while it was not significant in case of age and flexibility.

Lalithamma (1973) observed that creativity and age were positively and significantly related to each other.

Khire (1971) and Badrinath and Satya Narayana (1979) reported that creativity increases upto the age of 13 years.

Joshi (1974) and Gakhar (1974) found that creativity increases upto the age of 15 years.

Sansanwal and Jarial (1980) observed a consistent increase in the verbal fluency, originality and total verbal creativity of the students from 12 to 16 years age but the beyond the age of 16 years there was a decrease in the above mentioned components of creativity.

Ahmed (1980) reported a significant development in the verbal and non-verbal creativity from classes VII to XI.

Passi (1971) and Thammaprateep (1976) found a negative relationship between age and creativity.

Vohra (1975) observed a negative relationship between non-verbal creativity and age among primary school students.

Singh (1978) observed the same relationship between creativity and age among teacher trainees.

Rawat and Agrawal (1977) reported that from 12 to 16 years age creativity was negatively related with age in case of boys, whereas, the relationship between these two variables was positive in case of girls.

Jain (1975) and Bhargava (1979) reported that there exists no relationship between creativity and age.

2. Creative Thinking and Birth Order

Srivastave (1978) and Jarial (1979, 1981) found that first born were superior to later born with respect to different components of verbal creativity.

Jarial (1981) found that second born were superior to fourth born and fifth born in verbal fluency, and to fifth born in verbal flexibility, originality and total creativity. Third born were superior to fifth born in different components of verbal creativity, the fourth born were superior to fifth born in originality and total creativity and the seventh born were superior to fifth born in flexibility.

Srivastava (1977), Srivastava (1978) and Badrinath and Satya Narayana (1979) reported to no significant differences in the verbal creativity of students of different birth orders.

3. Creative Thinking and Sex

Boys show greater creativity than girls, especially as childhood advances, in large part, this is due to the different treatment boys and girls receive. Boys are given more opportunities to be independent, they are prodded by peers to take more risks, and they are encouraged by parents and teachers to show more initiative and originality. As Torrance has explained, "There is little doubt that the attitudes and treatment accorded girls and women by a society influence their creative development and behaviour".

Passi (1971), Bedi (1974), Singh (1975), Rawat and Garg (1977), Arora (1978), and Jarial (1981) found that female students were significantly superior to male students on verbal creativity.

Bedi (1974) and Jarial (1981), Hussain (1974) and Pandit (1976) reported that females were significantly superior to males on fluency, flexibility and originality dimensions of creativity.

Raina (1971) and Goyal (1973) found that females were significantly superior to males only on fluency and flexibility-dimensions of creativity.

Female students were, also, found to be superior to male students in originality dimension of creativity (Hussain and Hussain, 1975 and Jarial and Sharma, 1981).

Male students were found to be significantly superior to their female counterparts on verbal creativity (Prakash, 1966; Gangneja, 1972; Jain, 1975; Rawat and Agrawal, 1977; Badrinath and Satyanarayan, 1979; and Sharma, 1979).

On the non-verbal creativity too, the male students were significantly superior to female students (Passi, 1971).

With respect to different dimensions of creativity, it was reported that male students were significantly higher than female students on originality (Raina, 1971; Dhir, 1973; Awasthry, 1979; and Badrinath and Satya Narayana, 1979); on fluency (Awasthy, 1979 and Jarial and Sharma, 1981); on fluency and originality (Pandey, 1980); and on elaboration (Singh, 1978).

Boys were better than girls in verbal and non-verbal creative thinking ability (Trimurthy, 1987; Bogayata, 1986; Sharma, K, 1982).

Male students scored significantly than female students in all measures of verbal and figural creativity (Dharmangandan, 1981).

No significant differences were found between male and female students with respect to verbal creativity (Raina, 1970; Gakhr, 1974; Thammaprateep, 1976; Dutt, et.al., 1977; Lal, 1977; Singh, 1977; Throat, 1977; Singh, 1978; Gupta, 1979; Masih, 1979; and Pandy, 1980).

Vohra (1975) found that male and female students of primary grade did not differ significantly on non-verbal creativity.

No significant difference in mean creative thinking scores was found between males and females (Chaudary, 1983).

Vora Gira (1984) found no significant difference between the means of both sexes after taking divergent thinking programme in Mathematics.

Adolescent creativity is clearly sex sensitive (Chauhan, 1984). Dasai (1987) found no sex difference in creativity.

Gupta (1985) found creative training programme equally affects both male and female students.

4. Creative Thinking and Locality

The children from urban environments tend to be more creative than children from rural environments. Authoritarian training is more common in rural homes, and rural environment offers less stimulation to creativity than the larger environments of cities and their suburbs.

As early as 1969 a study was conducted by Aaron, Marihal and Malatesha where they explored the differences on creativity among rural an urban students. These investigators came to the conclusion that there existed no significant difference in creativity among students coming from rural and urban areas.

Sehgal (1978), Bhogayata (1986) and Desai (1987) also reported the similar finding. But Sharma (1972, 1974) reported that rural students were significantly more creative than urban students. On the other hand, studies conducted by Passi (1971), Singh (1977), Srivastava (1978), Singh (1979), Singh, G. (1985), and Trimurthry (1987) reported the superiority of urban students over rural students in creativity.

5. Creative Thinking and Socio-economic Status

Children of the higher socio-economic groups tend to be more creative than those of the lower groups. The former, for the most par, are brought up under democratic child-training methods, while the latter are far more likely to experience authoritarian training.

Democratic control fosters creativity by giving children more opportunities to express their individuality and pursue interests and activities of their own choosing. Even more important, the environment of children of the higher socio-economic groups provides more opportunities for gaining the knowledge and experience necessary for creativity. For example, young children from deprived homes have very few creative materials to play with and little encouragement to experiment with clay, paints, and puppets as compared with those from more favourable socio-economic environments.

Raina (1968), Vohra (1975), Gupta (1976), Rawat and Agarwal (1977), Singh (1977), Throat (1977), Singh (1978), Srivastava (1978), Awasthy(1979), Badrinadth and Satya Narayana (1979), Bargava (1979), Jarial (1979, 1981), Sahrma (1979, 1980), Ahmed (1980), Sharma and Jarial (1980), Singh (1980), and Vijaya Lakshmi (1980) studied creativity in relation to socio-economic status (SES). Most the studies reported that creative come from high SES (Vohra, 1975; Gupta, 1976; Rawat, and Agrawal, 1977; Singh, 1977; Throat, 1977; Singh, 1978; Srivastava, 1978; Jarial, 1979, 1980; Bhargava, 1979; Ahmed, 1980; Singh, 1980; and Vijaya Lakshmi, 1980) with respect to fluency component of creativity.

Sharma and Jarial (1980) observed that the students of high SES were superior to those of low SES.

Comparing the creativity scores of students coming from small, average and large families, Jarial (1981) and Agarwal (1982) found that the students of small families were significantly superior to the students of average and large families in fluency, flexibility and composite creativity, whereas, they did not differ with respect to originality as a component of creativity.

Few studies reported that creative come from average SES (Raina, 1968; and Awasthy, 1979). On the other hand, Das (1957), Lalitha (1957), Badrinath and Satya Narayana (1979), Seetharam and Vedanayagam (1979) and Chadha and Sen (1981) reported that there exists no significant differences in creativity of students coming from high, average and low SES.

Sharma and Jarial (1980) and Desai (1987) also reported that the students of high and low SES did not differ significantly in verbal flexibility, originality and total creativity.

6. Creative Thinking and Intelligence

Sharma, M. (1977) found males were superior to females, high and low creative males were significantly differentiated on intelligence.

Badrinath and Satya Narayana (1979) found the students of high intelligence group were significantly higher than the students of low intelligence group in creative thinking.

Sharma, K. (1982) found creativity was significantly higher in high IQ group to middle and low.

Sharma, S. C. (1979) found in high caste group, intelligence was related with verbal originality and composite verbal creativity but not in the low caste.

Patel, R. P. (1988) found students of experimental group did better on creativity test after the treatment than the students of the controlled group. Patel, J.Z (1987) observed the same.

V. Ryal Michael (1988) found that creative thinking ability was affected by IQ.

Awasthy, M. (1979), Rawat, M. S. and Agarwal (1977) found intelligence was significantly related to fluency and total creativity of the students.

Gupta, P. K (1985) found no significant interaction among the level of intelligence and creative training programme.

Ghaka, Paramjit and Pushpa (1980) found no significant difference between originality of the students of high, average and low intelligence.

7. Creative Thinking and Interest

Pal, A. (1980) showed the difference between two socio-economic groups were significant and the same found in both male and female students.

Sharma, S.C. (1979) found no significant association between interest and verbal creative functioning.

8. Creative Thinking and Adolescence

Paramesh, C. R. (1970) found high creative adolescents were neither more nor less introverts than the low and moderate creative adolescents.

Chauhan, Y. (1984) found social cultural plane, sex and frustration on psycho-social plane appeared highly contributing to promotion and demotion of components of adolescent creativity were clearly sex sensitivity.

9. Creative Thinking and Neuroticism

Paramesh, C. R. (1970) reported high creative adolescents were not different from low and moderate creative individuals in neuroticism.

V. Ryal Michael (1988) found creative thinking ability was affected by neuroticism.

Nathavat, S. S. (1977) found that high creative individuals were not different from the low and moderate creative individuals.

Desai, N.N. (1987) reported that students of low neuroticism level were more creative.

Srivastava, B. (1982) reported no significant difference on high and low creative individuals.

10. Creative Thinking and Scholastic Achievements

Sharma, M. (1977) reported that males were superior to females, high and low creative males were significantly differentiated on scholastic achievements.

Desai, N.N. (1987) found that the students with higher scholastic achievement were found better in creative thinking than students with low scholastic achievement. But no difference was found in urban and rural higher secondary students.

Sharma, K. (1982) found a positive relation to the measures of creativity and scholastic achievement.

Awasthy, M. (1979) reported that scholastic areas of creativity were significantly related to fluency and total creativity of the students.

Rajagopalan, S. (1988) found achievement motivation had no effect on the level of creativity of the students.

11. Creative Thinking and Anxiety

Sharma, M. (1977) reported that males were superior to females, high and low creative males were significantly differentiated in anxiety.

Desai, N. N. (1987) found that the students with higher anxiety were found better in creative thinking than students with low anxiety. But no difference was found in urban and rural higher secondary students.

V. Ryar Michael (1988) found that creative thinking ability programme was affected by anxiety level of the students of grades V, VI and VII.

Arora, G.L. (1976) found that anxiety was curvilinear related to creative thinking ability of male teacher trainees.

Paramesh, C.R. (1970) reported that high creative individuals were not different from low and moderate creative individuals in their anxiety level.

Natjawat, S. S. (1977) found that high creative individuals were not different from moderate and low creative individuals in free-floating anxiety, observation, phobic anxiety and somatic anxiety.

12. Creative Thinking and Risk Taking

Sharma, M. (1977) reported that males were superior in creativity to females but low risk taking.

Agrawal, S. (1982) found that risk taking more or less was found to be a positive and significant factor in fostering creativity of both the sexes.

13. Creative Thinking and Home

Sharma, M. (1977) reported that males were superior in creativity to females; high and low creative males were significantly differentiated in home conditions.

Sharma, K. (1982) found creativity was higher in nuclear families and families with higher SES.

Ahmed, S. (1980) found a significant difference in the verbal and non-verbal creativity of the students coming from advantaged and disadvantaged home backgrounds.

Aggarwal, S. (1982) found that home played no role or very significant role in fostering creativity of the both the sexes.

Nathawat, S.S. (1977) reported no significant difference among the high, the moderate and the low creative individuals. Srivastava, B. (1982) and Upadyaya, R. (1982) found the same.

14. Creative Thinking and Reasoning Ability

Desai, N.N. (1987) found no difference in creative thinking ability of urban and rural higher secondary students on reasoning ability; and students with good reasoning ability were better in creative thinking than the students with poor reasoning ability.

Sharma, S.C. (1979) found non-verbal reasoning was not related to verbal creative functioning in any of the caste groups.

15. Creative Thinking and Self-awareness

Sami, S. (1986) found that different dimensions of creativity were positive and significant of university students on self-awareness.

Nathawat, S. S. (1977) reported high creative individuals were not found different from the low and moderate creative individuals on health. Srivastava, B. (1982) also found the same.

Sharma, S. C. (1979) reported no significant association of creative thinking with illness.

16. Creative Thinking and Health

Sharma, M. (1977) found that males were superior to females; high and low creative males were significantly differentiated on health.

17. Creative Thinking and Self-adjustment

Sami, S. (1986) found that different dimensions of creativity were positive and significant of university students on self-adjustment.

Kaur, R. (1980) found a negative but low and insignificant relationship between creativity and adjustment.

18. Creative Thinking and Self-concept

Bhogayata, C. K. (1986) reported that boys were more creative than girls on self-concept.

19. Creative Thinking and Emotional Adjustment

Desai, N. N. (1982) reported that the students with high emotional stability were better in creative thinking than students with low emotional stability.

Sharma, M. (1977) found that males were superior in creativity to females; high creative males were significantly differentiated on emotional adjustment.

Nathawat, S. S. (1977) reported that the high creative individuals were not different from the low and moderate creative individuals on emotional adjustment.

Srivastava, B. (1982) found no significant difference among high, moderate and low creative individuals on emotional adjustment.

V. Ryal Michael (1988) found that creative thinking ability was effective on emotional stability.

20. Creative Thinking and Academic Achievement

Asha, C. B. (1980) found a positive and significant relationship between creativity and achievement scores of male as well as female students.

Badrinath, S. and Satya Narayana, S.B. (1979), Sharma, A.K. found no significant difference in the creativity of the students of low, middle and high academic achievement groups.

21. Creative Thinking and Parental Condition

Sharma, M. (1977) reported that female□fs creativity and parent education were significantly associated; and high creative females were significantly high than low creative females.

Dubey and Sushma (1986) found a significant positive mean effect on creative thinking in children of parent education.

Bindal, V.R. (1984) found a significant relationship between various components of creativity and pupils' perception of parents' attitude towards creativity.

V. Ryar Michael (1988) reported that creative thinking ability was effective on parental behaviour for student's grades V, VI and VII.

Sharma, S. C. (1979) found no significant association between creativity and parental education.

22. Creative Thinking and Personality Factor

Kundu, D. (1984) reported that males had higher scores in creativity than females on personality factors.

Upadhyaya, R. (1982) showed that the personality of a creative child is similar to that of an adult creative.

Vohara, I.N. (1975) found no significant combination between non-verbal creativity and personality characteristics.

Nathawat, S.S. (1977) found that the high creative individuals were not different from low and moderate creative individuals in personality traits.

23. Creative Thinking and School Environment

Rajagopalan, S. (1988) found that class room climate is conducive to the growth of creative talent.

Sharma, K. (1982) found that central school students were most creative, next in order were public, private-aided and government schools respectively; and organisational climate of the school was not to be related to creativity in students.

V. Ryral Michael (1988) reported that creative thinking ability was affected by school achievements.

Dubey and Sushma (1986) reported that school environment has a significant positive main effect on creative thinking in children.

Gupta, A.K. (1977) found no significant difference between the pupils studying institutions with different types of institutional climate with respect to their scores on composite creativity, but significant relationship between verbal creativity and teaching verbal behaviour.

Nathawat, S. S. (1977) reported that the high creative individuals were not found different from the low and moderate creative individual on school. The same was also observed by Srivastava, B. (1982).

24. Creative Thinking and Psychological Factors

Kundu, D. (1984) found that males had higher scores on originality than females, and males evinced greater psychoticism than females.

Sharma, K. (1982) reported that boys were more creative as compared to girls in terms of psychological factors.

25. Creative Thinking and Ego-strength

Kundu, D. (1984) reported that males had higher scores than females on ego-strength.

Srivastava, B. (1982) found that the high creative individuals were significantly higher positive ego-strength than the low and moderate creative individual.

26. Creative Thinking and Security Feelings

Nathawat, S.S. (1977) reported that the high creative individuals were not found different from the low and moderate creative individual on security feelings.

27. Creative Thinking and Values

Pal, A. (1980) reported no significant difference in two socio-economic groups and the result was true for both male and female students.

Singh, L. and Gupta, G. (1977) reported a significant positive relationship between the creativity and aesthetic value of science girls.

Man, G.S. (1978) found high creative boys and high creative girls did not differ from each other in aesthetic value and same observed in low creative boys and low creative girls.

28. Creative Thinking and Social Value

Singh, L. and Gupta, G. (1977) found significant negative relationship between the social values.

Srivastava, B. (1982) found no significant in social adjustment among the high, the moderate and the low creative individuals.

Sharma, S.C. (1979) found no significant association of creative thinking with social service.

Nathawat, S.S. (1977) reported that the high creative individuals were not found different from the low and moderate creative individual on social adjustment.

Upadhyaya, R. (1982) reported that social behaviour did not significantly relate to creativity.

29. Creative Thinking and Political Value

Singh, L. and Gupta, G. (1977) found science girls were significant and positive related to creativity over arts boys on political value.

30. Creative Thinking and Religious Value

Singh, L. and Gupta, G. (1977) found negative relationship between creativity and religious value of arts girls.

31. Creative Thinking and Intellectual Behaviour

Upadhyaya, R. (1982) reported that intellectual behaviour of children was significantly correlated with creativity.

32. Creative Thinking and Mathematics

Bhagwat, S.A. (1992) reported that divergent thinking abilities were developed by using the divergent production type problems in Mathematics in both boys and girls.

Biswal, J. (1988) found that pupils f creativity in Mathematics is a linear function of each of the variables (SHM and PPTM).

Vora, Gira (1984) reported that creativity increased as a result of treatment of divergent thinking programme in Mathematics (DTPM) both in boys and girls.

34. Creative Thinking and Science and Arts

Awasthy, M. (1979) showed science students were significantly higher than arts students in fluency and flexibility areas of creativity.

Rawat, M. S. and Garg, M.K. (1977) found no significant difference in creativity of students of arts and science faculties.

35. Creative Thinking and Languages (Mother Tongue)

Badrinath and Satya Narayanana, S.B. (1979) found no difference in creativity scores of the students speaking different languages (mother tongue).

The above review of the related research developed a clear insight in selecting the present problem as the review does not reflect any study exactly suitable to the present study.

3

DESIGN OF THE RESEARCH

The formidable problem that follows the task of defining the research problem is the preparation of the design of the research project, popularly known as the 'Research Design'.

A research design is the arrangement of conditions for collection and analysis of data in a manner that aims to combine relevance to research purpose with economy in procedure (Clair Selltiz, *et.al.*, 1962).

In fact, the research design is the conceptual structure within which research is conducted. Important features of a research design are: it is a plan that specifies the source and types of information relevant to the research problem; it is a strategy specifying which approach will be used for gathering and analysing the data; and it also includes the time and cost budgets since most studies are done under these two constraints.

Research design is needed because it facilitates the smooth sailing of various research operations, thereby making research as efficient as possible yielding maximal information with minimal expenditure of effort, time and money.

Research design stands for advanced planning of the methods to be adopted for collecting the relevant data and the techniques to be used in their analysis, keeping in view the objectives of the research and the availability of staff, time and money. Research design, in fact, has a great bearing on the reliability of the results arrived at and as such it constitutes the firm foundation of the entire edifice of the research work.

Planning is a necessary step for a good research as it is the heart of any research. In this chapter, the following aspects have been discussed in detail, which are concerned with the design of the present study. Research procedures followed include the operational definitions of the different terms used, the various hypotheses that were framed for verification and the rationale of these hypotheses. Selection of the sample includes the sampling techniques used, the reasons for selection of a particular sampling technique, and the selection of sample according to different variables. Selection of research tool covers selection of collection of data, description of tool selected, testing its suitability for the present study and the procedure followed in the administration of the tool to collect the data required for this study.

OPERATIONAL DEFINITIONS OF KEY TERMS

The operational definitions of the important terms used in the present study entitled "A Study of Creative Thinking of Secondary School Students" are discussed and defined herewith:

1. ***Study:*** Comprehensive awareness of anything;
2. ***Creative thinking***: It is either mental or physical activity of thinking that performs something new from already existing ideas;
3. ***Secondary schools:*** Schools (in 10+2+3 pattern of education) with VIII, IX, X classes are known as secondary schools;
4. ***Government Schools:*** The secondary schools under the management of government officials are called government schools. So, schools managed by the government, municipalities, zilla parishads are government schools;

5. *Private Schools:* The secondary schools managed by the private organisations or persons either partially or totally are considered as private schools. The government recognised and government aided schools managed by private managements are to be considered as private schools;

6. *Rural Schools:* The schools located in rural areas (villages) are called rural schools.

7. *Urban Schools:* The schools located in urban areas (towns and cities) are known as urban schools;

8. *English Medium Schools:* The schools where the medium of instruction is in English language are called English medium schools;

9. *Telugu Medium Schools:* The schools where the medium of instruction is in Telugu language are called Telugu medium schools.

VARIABLES OF THE STUDY

Variables are necessary requisites for any worthwhile research for the purpose of comparison. They are the conditions or characteristics that the researcher manipulates, controls or observes in the behavioural science. These variables must be defined operationally by describing some samples of actual behaviour that are concrete enough to be observed directly.

For the present study, the following variables are considered:

1. *Management:* Government versus private school students;

2. *Location:* Rural versus urban school students;

3. *Medium of Instruction:* Telugu medium versus English medium students;

4. *Gender:* Boys versus girls.

The following is the rationale for selecting the above said variables:

1. Government versus Private Secondary School Students

The reputation of private schools is generally considered superior when compared with that of government schools. Private school students are exposed to better study atmosphere with the facilities like laboratories, libraries, etc. The quality of teaching is also supposed to be better. Since the standards of teaching and the physical facilities are supposed to be different in private and government schools, the creative thinking of students may be different. So, this variable has been taken up to study the difference in the level of creative thinking of private and government secondary school students.

2. Rural versus Urban Secondary School Students

Urban schools are well equipped in many aspects when compared with rural schools. The facilities like buildings, libraries, laboratories, teaching staff, educational atmosphere, competitive spirit among pupils, exposure to workshops etc., are different from one to the other. These amenities provided to the school students may make them to develop better creative thinking. So, this variable has been taken up for consideration.

3. Telugu Medium versus English Medium Secondary School Students

Medium of instruction is taken as a variable to see if any significant difference is there in the creative thinking between Telugu medium and English medium school students as the expression capacity is different in both the cases due to their language use and ability.

4. Boy versus Girl Students

Gender is taken as a variable to observe difference between boys and girls in their creative thinking as several psychological aspects of boys and girls differ significantly.

HYPOTHESES OF THE STUDY

Hypothesis is a shrewd and intelligent guess, supposition, hunch, provisional statement or tentative generalisation as to the existence of some fact, condition or relationship relative to some phenomenon, which serves to explain already known facts in a given area of research and to guide the search for new truth on the basis of empirical evidence. The hypothesis is put to test for its tenability and to determine its validity.

For the present study, the following hypotheses are formulated:

Hypothesis 1

The secondary school students are not holding a high level of creative thinking.

Hypothesis 2

There is no significant difference in the creative thinking of secondary school girls and boys.

Hypothesis 3

There is no significant difference in the creative thinking of urban and rural secondary school students.

Hypothesis 4

There is no significant difference in the creative thinking of English medium and Telugu medium secondary school students.

Hypothesis 5

There is no significant difference in the creative thinking of government and private secondary school students.

Hypothesis 6

There is no significant difference in the creative thinking of urban secondary school girls and boys.

Hypothesis 7

There is no significant difference in the creative thinking of rural secondary school girls and boys.

Hypothesis 8

There is no significant difference in the creative thinking of urban English medium and Telugu medium secondary school students.

Hypothesis 9

There is no significant difference in the creative thinking of rural English medium and Telugu medium secondary school students.

Hypothesis 10

There is no significant difference in the creative thinking of rural Telugu medium secondary school girls and boys.

Hypothesis 11

There is no significant difference in the creative thinking of rural English medium secondary school girls and boys.

Hypothesis 12

There is no significant difference in the creative thinking of urban Telugu medium secondary school girls and boys.

Hypothesis 13

There is no significant difference in the creative thinking of urban English medium secondary school girls and boys.

SAMPLE OF THE STUDY

A sample is a small proportion of a population selected for observation and analysis. It is a collection consisting of a part or subset of the objects or individuals of population that is selected for the express purpose of representing the population. By observing the characteristics of the sample, one can make certain inferences about the characteristics of the population from which it is drawn.

After finalising the variables, consideration was given to whether the entire population is to be made the subject for data collection or a particular group is to be selected as representative of the whole population. The entire population here refers to all the eighth class students studying in secondary schools of Nellore district.

The selection of a group as a representative of the whole population was found to be more convenient and suitable. The technique leads to a considerable saving of time, effort and finance. The number of students selected will be small in order to make a detailed and intensive study. This generally leads to more accurate and reliable results. As this sampling has many advantages it was selected for the collection of data.

In any social research, various methods are utilised for selection and drawing of samples. After a detailed study of all these methods and considering the variables selected for the research work, the stratified sampling technique was found to be most suitable.

In stratified sampling technique, the entire population is divided into two smaller homogeneous groups and then the sample is selected within each group. Every sampling unit in the population is placed in one of the strata prior to the selection of the sample so that the sum of the strata is identical with the population. Stratified sampling method has certain merits and advantages as a technique of sampling. Auckoff has rightly said that stratified sampling enables the researcher to make a comparison of properties of the strata as well as to estimate population characteristics.

In stratified sampling technique, the investigator has greater control over the selection of the sample when compared with random sampling. In random sampling technique although every group has a chance of being selected and included in the sample there is every possibility and sometimes it does happen that certain important groups are left unrepresented. But, in stratified sampling technique, no important group is likely to be left out.

Stratified sampling is the ideal one when comparison between different variables has to be made. For example, if comparison has to be made between private and government school students or rural and urban school students, it would be very difficult to select the required number of units through any other technique of sampling. If any other technique is used, the problem of bias and prejudice creeps in.

Replacement of units is also possible in the stratified sampling technique. Normally, if a particular unit is not accessible for a study, it is difficult to replace it by any other technique but in this technique it is possible. Stephen states that stratification automatically brings about a replacement of persons lost to the sample by persons of the same stratum, thus partly correcting the bias that would result if there were no replacement of units. As the entire population is divided into particular strata it is easy and convenient to replace an inaccessible case by an accessible one.

In stratified sampling technique, much depends on the stratification process. The following precautions were taken while stratifying the population; the variables involved in the study were taken note of; care was taken to see that each stratum in the universe was large enough in size so that the selection of items could be done on random basis; the strata formed were definite and clear cut; each stratum was free from influence of the other so that there would be no overlapping.

Before actually selecting the sample, certain fundamental principles were considered to make the sample scientific and clear-cut.

Firstly, the 'universe' was clearly defined. In the technical phraseology of research, the whole population out of which the samples are selected is known as the 'universe'. For the present research work, the universe includes all the students of eighth class studying in secondary schools of Nellore district. The study was limited to a particular geographical area to facilitate appropriate sample selection and to avoid bias and prejudice.

Secondly, decision has to be made about the units of the sample. A unit of sample may be a house, a family, a group of individuals or a single individual. A good unit should possess these characteristics. (1) *Clarity:* The unit should be clearly defined in unambiguous terms. This would make the study easy and efficient. For the present research work, a sampling unit was defined as a student of eighth class studying in any secondary school of Nellore district. (2) *Suitability:* A good unit should be well suited to the problem under study. Since the problem is the reasoning ability of ninth class pupils of Nellore district, the unit selected is well suited to the problem. (3) *Accessibility:* The unit selected should be easily accessible to the researcher. If the units selected are difficult to reach and if the researcher fails to make use of them, the study would be vitiated. The selected sample unit, i.e., eighth class student studying in secondary schools is easily accessible since he/she could be approached in any secondary school.

Thirdly, consideration should be given to the preparation of the source list. This is an important factor that makes representative selection possible. A source list is the list which contains the names of the units of the universe from which the sample may be selected. It may exist even before the beginning of the project or it may be prepared afresh by the investigator himself. Without a source list, study through a sampling technique is not possible. For the present research work, a source list consisting of the names of schools in Nellore district was used. Care was taken to see that the source list was up-to-date and valid and that there was no repetition of names of the schools. This source list was found to be relevant and suitable because it included secondary schools as the study deals with the eighth class students of secondary schools.

Besides considering these principles, it is extremely important to think about the size of the sample to be selected. If the sample is either too small or too large, it will make the study difficult and also make the results untenable. According to Patten, 'an optimum sample in survey is one which fulfills the requirements of effective representativeness, reliability and flexibility'. The sample should be small enough to avoid intolerable sampling error.

The size of the sample for the present research work was decided after considering the following factors.

Since an intensive study was planned, a very large number of samples were not selected. In case of an intensive study, very large number of samples was not as useful as it involves huge consumption of resources. A smaller sample was most convenient.

The size and selection of the samples will also be influenced by the nature of the universe. If the universe is homogeneous, even a small-sized sample may yield dependable and required results. If the universe is heterogeneous, small-sized samples may not be useful. In case of the present study, the heterogeneous universe was split into smaller homogeneous strata and the samples were selected from these strata.

The investigators need to determine the number of groups to be formed. In case the number of groups proposed is large, the size of the samples shall have to be large so that every group should be of proper size and suit the requirements of the study. In case the number of groups proposed is small, even small-sized samples can fulfill the requirement. In case of the present study, the number of groups into which the universe was divided is—girls and boys, private and government school students, rural and urban school students, English medium and Telugu medium school students. Since the number of groups was moderate, a reasonable sample was selected from each of these groups.

The size of the sample is also governed by the size of the tools to be used. In case the tools are short and the questions asked pertain to certain limited factors, a large sample can be selected. In case the tools are large and the questions are complicated, the sample should be small in size so that, from administrative point of view, the investigator may not be put to unnecessary troubles. In the present study, the tool was quite elaborate and implicit; hence a very large sample was not selected.

The sampling technique also determines the size of the sample. When random sampling technique is used, the samples have to be large. On the other hand, if samples are selected through stratified sampling technique, the reliability can be achieved even with the help of the small-sized samples.

After taking into consideration all these factors, which influence the size of the sample, it was decided that an ideal sample would consist of two hundred students. This sample is small enough to avoid intolerable sampling errors and large enough to draw perfect conclusions.

After deciding about the sampling method and the size of the sample, the universe was divided into different strata. The variables chosen for the study were considered to divide the universe. The variables chosen were boys versus girls, government versus private secondary school students, rural versus urban secondary school students, English medium versus Telugu medium secondary school students.

Following the above sampling procedure, 200 eighth class students were selected as sample for the present study. The total sample of 200 eighth class students consists of the following number of variables: Boys - 100; Girls - 100; Private school students - 100; Government school students - 100; Rural school students - 100; Urban school students - 100; English medium school students - 100; Telugu medium school students - 100.

The sampling design employed thus involved not only stratification of the universe but also random sampling technique to select samples from with in the stratum.

TOOL OF THE STUDY

A research tool plays an important role in any worthwhile research as it is the sole factor in determining the sound data and in arriving at perfect conclusions about the problem on hand, which ultimately helps in providing suitable remedial measures to the problem concerned.

The selection and use of tools can be done in two ways. The first one is to construct a tool independently by the researcher for his study. Here, there are many problems in doing so.

The second way of selection and use of tools is right selection of tools from already standardised ones available in the field of study. Here also, it involves a tedious job in locating the tools and identifying their usefulness to the study on hand.

Considering the merits and limitations of the selection of tools, the researcher is interested in using "Non-Verbal Test of Creative Thinking" constructed and standardised by Bacquer Mehdi.

The non-verbal test of creative thinking is intended to measure the individual's ability to deal with figural content in a creative manner. Three types of activity are used for this purpose, viz., picture construction, picture completion, and triangles and ellipses. The total time required for administering the test is 35 minutes, in addition to the time necessary for giving instructions, passing out booklets and collecting them back.

Administration of the Test

The test has been personally administered on the secondary school students taking all the necessary precautions.

4

ANALYSIS OF THE DATA

The next step in the process of research, after the collection of data, is the organisation, analysis and interpretation of data and formulation of conclusions and generalisations to get a meaningful picture out of the raw information collected. The analysis and interpretation of data involves the objective material in the possession of the researcher and his subjective reactions and desires to be derived from the data, the inherent meanings in their relation to the problem (Rummel, 1958).

Analysis of data means studying the organised material in order to discover inherent facts. The data are studied from as many angles as possible to explore the new facts. Analysis requires an alert, flexible and open mind. It is worthwhile to prepare a plan of analysis before the actual collection of data. Good, Barr and Scates (1941) suggest four helpful modes to get started on analysing the gathered data. They are: 1. To think in terms of significant tables that the data permit; 2. To examine carefully the statement of the problem and earlier analysis and to study the original records of the data; 3. To get away from the data and to think about the problem of layman's terms, or to actually discuss that problem with others; 4. To attack the data by making various statistical calculations.

The mass data collected through the use of research tool need to be systematised and organised, i.e., edited, classified and tabulated before it can serve the purpose. Here, editing implies the checking of gathered data for accuracy, utility and completeness; classifying refers to dividing the information into different categories, classes or heads, for use; and tabulating denotes the recording of the classified material in accurate mathematical terms.

To measure the level of creative thinking possessed by each sub-sample as well as the whole sample, the total score of creative thinking of each student is taken into consideration. There are three activities in the test. In Activity-I, there are 2 items; in Activity-II, there are 10 items and in activity-III, there are 14 items, and totally there are 26 items. The minimum and maximum score weight of Activity-I are 1 and 5, Activity-II are 2 and 5, and Activity-III are 1 and 5 respectively according to the norms of the tool. Therefore, low score of creative thinking is 36 and high score of creative thinking is 130.

Interpretation of Scores of Creative Thinking

S. No.	*Score*	*Interpretation*
1.	36-55	Very Low Creative Thinking`
2.	56-85	Low Creative Thinking
3.	86-105	High Creative Thinking
4.	105-130	Very High Creative Thinking

For the purpose of classification of the level of creative thinking possessed by the sample: who scored 36 to 55 are very low creative, 56 to 85 are low creative, 86 to 105 are high creative and 106 to 130 are of very high creative group. This classification was considered as eighth class students are in the age group of 12 to 13 years.

The t-test was used for testing the significance of hypotheses.

Hypothesis-1

"The secondary school students are not holding a high level of creative thinking."

To test the validity of hypothesis-1, the mean value of the whole sample is calculated.

Table 4.1

Creative Thinking of Secondary School Students

Sample	*Sample Size*	*Mean*	*Standard Deviation*
Secondary School Students	200	89.46	13.25

As per the mean value obtained in Table 4.1, the secondary school students are holding a high level of creative thinking.

The hypothesis that "the secondary school students are not holding a high level of creative thinking" can be accepted.

Hypothesis-2

"There is no significant difference in the creative thinking of secondary school girls and boys".

To test the validity of the above hypothesis, the mean and the standard deviation along with t- test are calculated and results are tabulated as follows.

Table 4.2

Creative Thinking of Boys and Girls of Secondary Schools

Variable	*Sample Size*	*Mean*	*S.D.*	*σ D*	*t*
Girls	100	87.64	14.21	1.86	1.99*
Boys	100	91.35	11.94		

* Significant at 0.05 level.

As per the scores obtained in Table 4.2, the mean value of girls is 87.64 and of the boys is 91.35, which fall in high creative thinking category. Boys are more creative thinkers than girls. The t-value of girls and boys is 1.99 which is significant at 0.05 level. Boys are more creative in thinking than their counterparts.

The hypothesis that "there is no significant difference in the creative thinking of secondary school girls and boys" can be rejected.

Hypothesis-3

"There is no significant difference in the creative thinking of urban and rural secondary school students".

To test the validity of the above hypothesis, the following calculations are done and the results are tabulated as follows:

Table 4.3

Creative Thinking of Rural and Urban Secondary School Students

Variable	*Sample Size*	*Mean*	*S.D.*	*σ D*	*t*
Urban	100	92.26	12.56	1.85	2.40*
Rural	100	87.83	13.54		

* Significant at 0.05 level.

As per the scores obtained in Table 4.3, the mean value of urban students is 92.26 and of rural students is 87.83. Though both of them are holding high creative thinking ability, urban students are more creative thinkers than rural students. The t-value of urban and rural students is 2.40, which is significant at 0.05 level.

The hypothesis that "there is no significant difference in the creative thinking of urban and rural secondary school students" can be rejected.

Hypothesis-4

"There is no significant difference in the creative thinking of English medium and Telugu medium secondary school students".

To test the validity of the above hypothesis, following calculations are attended:

Table 4.4

Creative Thinking of English Medium and Telugu Medium Secondary School Students

Variable	*Sample Size*	*Mean*	*S.D.*	*σ D*	*t*
English Medium	100	91.98	12.05	1.82	2.29*
Telugu Medium	100	87.82	13.63		

* Significant at 0.05 level.

As per the values shown in the Table 4.4, the mean value of English medium students is 91.98 and of Telugu medium students is 87.82. Even though both of them fall in high creative thinking category, English medium students are more creative thinkers than Telugu medium students. The t-value of English medium and Telugu medium students is 2.29, which is significant at 0.05 level.

The hypothesis that "there is no significant difference in the creative thinking of English medium and Telugu medium secondary school students" can be rejected.

Hypothesis-5

"There is no significant difference in the creative thinking of government and private secondary school students".

To test the validity of the above hypothesis, the mean, standard deviation and t- values are calculated.

Table 4.5
Creative Thinking of Private and Government Secondary School Students

Variable	*Sample Size*	*Mean*	*S.D.*	*σ D*	*t*
Government Students	100	87.64	14.21	1.86	2.00*
Private Students	100	91.35	11.94		

* Significant at 0.05 level.

As per the values in the Table 4.5, the mean value of government school students is 87.64 and of private school students is 91.35. Though both of them are in high creative thinking category, the private school students are more creative thinkers than the government school students. The t-value of government and private school students is 1.99 that is significant at 0.05 level.

The hypothesis that "there is no significant difference in the creative thinking of government and private secondary school students" can be rejected.

Hypothesis-6

"There is no significant difference in the creative thinking of urban secondary school girls and boys".

To test the validity of the above hypothesis, the calculations made are shown in the following table:

Table 4.6

Creative Thinking of Urban Secondary School Boys and Girls

Variable	*Sample Size*	*Mean*	*S.D.*	*σ D*	*t*
Girls	50	88.06	11.84	2.31	2.45*
Boys	50	93.26	11.26		

* Significant at 0.05 level.

As per the values in Table 4.6, the mean value of urban school girls is 88.06 and of urban school boys is 93.26. Though both the sub-samples hold a high creative thinking level, the urban school boys are more creative thinkers than the urban school girls. The t-value of urban girls and boys is 2.45, which is significant at 0.05 level.

The hypothesis that "there is no significant difference in the creative thinking of urban secondary school girls and boys" can be rejected.

Hypothesis-7

"There is no significant difference in the creative thinking of rural secondary school girls and boys".

To test the validity of the above hypothesis, following calculations are carried out:

Table 4.7

Creative Thinking of Rural Secondary School Girls and Boys

Variable	*Sample Size*	*Mean*	*S.D.*	*σ D*	*t*
Girls	50	85.22	14.77	2.66	1.96@
Boys	50	90.44	11.62		

@ Not Significant at 0.05 level.

As per the values in Table 4.7, the mean value of rural school girls is 85.22 and of rural school boys is 90.44. The t-value of girls and boys is 1.96, which is not significant.

The hypothesis that "there is no significant difference in the creative thinking of rural secondary school girls and boys" can be accepted.

Hypothesis-8

"There is no significant difference in the creative thinking of urban English medium and Telugu medium secondary school students".

To test the validity of the above hypothesis, the results are tabulated as follows:

Table 4.8

Creative Thinking of English and Telugu medium Urban Secondary School Students

Variable	*Sample Size*	*Mean*	*S.D.*	*σ D*	*t*
English Medium	50	95.34	12.11	2.41	3.47*
Telugu Medium	50	86.98	11.96		

* Significant at 0.05 level.

As per the values in Table 4.8, the mean value of urban English medium school students is 95.34 and of Telugu medium school students is 86.98. The urban English medium school students are more creative thinkers than urban Telugu medium school students. The t-value of urban E.M. and T.M. school students is 3.47, which is significant at 0.05 level.

The hypothesis that "there is no significant difference in the creative thinking of urban English medium and Telugu medium secondary school students" can be rejected.

Hypothesis-9

"There is no significant difference in the creative thinking of rural English medium and Telugu medium secondary school students".

To test the validity of the above hypothesis, the calculations made are tabulated as follows:

Table 4.9

Creative Thinking of Rural English and Telugu medium secondary School Students

Variable	*Sample Size*	*Mean*	*S.D.*	*σ D*	*t*
English Medium	50	89.98	14.22	2.59	2.12*
Telugu Medium	50	84.5	11.52		

* Significant at 0.05 level.

As per the values in Table 4.9, the mean value of rural English medium school students is 89.98 and of rural Telugu medium school students is 84.5. The rural English medium school students are better creative thinkers than rural Telugu medium school students. The t-value of rural English medium and Telugu medium secondary school students is 2.12, which is significant at 0.05 level.

The hypothesis that "there is no significant difference in the creative thinking of rural English medium and Telugu medium secondary school students" can be rejected.

Hypothesis-10

"There is no significant difference in the creative thinking of rural Telugu medium secondary school girls and boys".

To test the validity of the above hypothesis, the results are tabulated as follows:

Table 4.10

Creative Thinking of Rural Telugu medium Secondary School Girls and Boys

Variable	*Sample Size*	*Mean*	*S.D.*	*σ D*	*t*
Girls	25	85.92	17.08	4.12	1.31@
Boys	25	91.4	11.55		

@ Not Significant at 0.05 level.

As per the values in Table 4.10, the mean value of rural Telugu medium school girls is 85.92 and of boys is 91.4. The t-value of rural Telugu medium secondary school girls and boys is 1.3, which is not significant.

The hypothesis that "there is no significant difference in the creative thinking of rural Telugu medium secondary school girls and boys" can be accepted.

Hypothesis-11

"There is no significant difference in the creative thinking of rural English medium secondary school girls and boys".

To test the validity of the above hypothesis, the following calculations are made:

Table 4.11
Creative Thinking of Rural English Medium Secondary School Girls and Boys

Variable	*Sample Size*	*Mean*	*S.D.*	*σ D*	*t*
Girls	25	84.52	11.98	3.33	1.52@
Boys	25	89.48	11.01		

@ Not Significant at 0.05 level.

As per the values in Table 4.11, the mean value of rural English medium school girls is 84.52 and of rural English medium school boys is 89.48. The t-value of rural English medium school girls and boys is 1.52, which is not significant at 0.05 level.

The hypothesis that "there is no significant difference in the creative thinking of rural of English medium secondary school girls and boys" can be accepted.

Hypothesis-12

"There is no significant difference in the creative thinking of urban of Telugu medium secondary school girls and boys".

To test the validity of the above hypothesis, the calculations made are as follows:

Table 4.12

Creative Thinking of Urban Telugu Medium Secondary School Girls and Boys

Variable	*Sample Size*	*Mean*	*S.D.*	*σ D*	*t*
Girls	25	84.2	11.12	2.91	2.46*
Boys	25	91.36	9.41		

* Significant at 0.05 level.

As per the values in Table 4.12, the mean value of urban Telugu medium school girls is 84.2 and of boys is 91.36. The t-value of urban Telugu medium school girls and boys is 2.46, which is significant at 0.05 level. The boys have more creative thinking than their counterparts.

The hypothesis that "there is no significant difference in the creative thinking of urban Telugu medium secondary school girls and boys" can be rejected.

Hypothesis-13

"There is no significant difference in the creative thinking of urban English medium secondary school girls and boys".

To test the validity of the above hypothesis, results are tabulated as follows:

Table 4.13

Creative Thinking of Urban English Medium Secondary School Girls and Boys

Variable	*Sample Size*	*Mean*	*S.D.*	*σ D*	*t*
Girls	25	89.12	12.07	2.97	3.12*
Boys	25	98.36	8.67		

* Significant at 0.05 level.

As per the values in Table 4.13, the mean value of urban English medium school girls is 89.12 and of boys is 98.36. The urban English medium school boys are more creative thinkers than the urban

English medium school girls. The t-value of urban English medium school girls and boys is 3.12, which is significant at 0.05 level.

The hypothesis that "there is no significant difference in the creative thinking of urban of English medium secondary school girls and boys" can be rejected.

5

SUMMARY, CONCLUSIONS, DISCUSSION AND SUGGESTIONS

SUMMARY

Creative children are great assets to any progressing society. Development and progress in different areas of national life depends on creative children. Creativity is not restricted to the chosen few. All children are creative and its dimensions vary from child to child. It involves many traits: courage in conviction, independent in judgement, independent in thinking, intuitive in nature, vision for future, curiosity, originality, flexibility, fluency, emotional maturity, boldness, sensibility, tendency towards dominance, self-sufficiency and radicalness. Creativity is manifested through creative thinking, early in life and its development depends upon social conditions and conducive environment of the academic institution.

Since the days of Aristotle, it has been a common place to say that man differs from other animals, in that he is capable of thinking and reasoning. Thinking is of two kinds, viz., convergent thinking and divergent thinking. Convergent thinking leads to one solution to the problem, whereas divergent thinking leads to a number of solutions to the problem. Divergent thinking in other words called creative thinking. Coleridge insisted that the creative imagination is the supreme power in man. In the same way, Vein Leighton stated that 'man is not only an animal but a spiritual being and the greater difference between the two is man's power of creative imagination'.

Creative thinking is the very life blood of human civilisation. Our future depends upon creative thinking ability. Therefore creative thinking has become a chief psycho-social motive of the present generation. Creative thinking is more than a word today. It is an incantation. It is a kind of psychic wonder. It makes history through reshaping man's world.

Creative thinking requires newness, something unique, something better, some new association or addition to the old form or some new imagination. As Butcher (1972) observes, 'any society, to avoid stagnation, needs a constant supply of original ideas at all levels, but profoundly original men who are the most fertile source of these ideas are often the very people who most disturb the society by threatening its established ways of thought and familiar structure'.

Functioning of the mind and the nature of human genius has been the center of attention of psychologists and educationists for centuries. But it was not until very recently when Guilford propagated his theory of human intellect, that creative aspect of mental ability became the focus of research activity. Guilford's theory gave considerable impetus to recent research and theoretical interest in the area of creativity and creative education. The present popularity of the concept can in part, according to Cohen (1976) be accounted for in terms of changing fads and fashions, but a truer explanation of the current concern for creative thinking in schools probably lies elsewhere.

The systematic educational research in creative thinking is a relatively new field of endeavour. The problems are as complex, the concepts as uncertain, and the results often as conflicting as the subject. Whether it is about the relation between creativity and intelligence or between creative thinking and creative achievements, about threshold hypotheses, or about the possibility of facilitating creative thinking in the classroom, there seem to be almost as many points of view as there are studies. Inevitably one discovers the inadequacy of methodology of human research and the shortcomings in the techniques for studying creative thinking.

Given importance to creative thinking as an invaluable human resource for the development of any society or nation, it is but natural that many studies have been conducted, especially in the USA, on different aspects of creative thinking. Relationships between creative thinking and gender, age, location, socio-economic status, etc., are few examples of such studies. There is no gainsaying that the relationship between intelligence and creativity is the most controversial and most intriguing and challenging one to the researcher of intelligence and creativity.

Moreover, where adolescence is concerned, the literature on creativity has little to contribute except for general statements about it. One has to bridge the gap, trying to relate what he knows about adolescence to the statements about creativity. According to Arastesh and Arastesh (1976), creativity research and the development of talent have preceded from both childhood and adulthood with an obvious gap in the adolescent period. The recent concern with increasing scientific personnel has highlighted the need for fostering creative thinking endeavour at the high school level. Torrance (1964) commented that 'of the different educational levels, the high school years have been the most neglected in creativity research'.

What is necessary today is to bring about the optimum development of the whole individual. To realise this aim we will have to teach the child to think creatively about yet to be discovered (Crutchfield, 1967). Creativity is a naturally obtained boon to the man. Every one has creativity inherently in him without discrepancy of education, socio-economic status and heredity. Any one grows in his field that has both interest and creative thinking. Everyone has same number of hands, legs, organs, and 24 hours day, but those who improvise their creative thinking in their respective fields will be ahead of others. But, the thing is we have to identify, sharpen and promote it. Curiosity gives colours to creative thinking. Creative thinking gives variety from monotony of life.

Hence, the problem selected for the present investigation was "A Study of Creative Thinking of Secondary School Students". The study was aimed at analysing the creative thinking of students of secondary schools in relation to certain variables like gender of the sampling unit, locality of the school, medium of instruction in the school and management of the school.

The present study was planned to proceed with the following objectives: 1. To assess the level of creative thinking of secondary school students; 2. To study the creative thinking of boys and girls of secondary schools; 3. To study the creative thinking of rural and urban secondary school students; 4. To study the creative thinking of Telugu medium and English medium secondary school students; 5. To study the creative thinking of government and private secondary school students.

Based on the above objectives, the following hypotheses were formulated for investigation: 1. The secondary school students are not holding a high level of creative thinking; 2. There is no significant difference in the creative thinking of secondary school girls and boys; 3. There is no significant difference in the creative thinking of urban and rural secondary school students; 4. There is no significant difference in the creative thinking of English medium and Telugu medium secondary school students; 5. There is no significant difference in the creative thinking of government and private secondary school students; 6. There is no significant difference in the creative thinking of urban secondary school girls and boys; 7. There is no significant difference in the creative thinking of rural secondary school girls and boys; 8. There is no significant difference in the creative thinking of urban English medium and Telugu medium secondary school students; 9. There is no significant difference in the creative thinking of rural English medium and Telugu medium secondary school students; 10. There is no significant difference in the creative thinking of rural Telugu medium secondary school girls and boys; 11. There is no significant difference in the creative thinking of rural English medium secondary school girls and boys; 12. There is no significant difference in the creative thinking of urban Telugu medium secondary school girls and boys; 13. There is no significant difference in the creative thinking of urban English medium secondary school girls and boys.

The variables chosen for the present study were: 1. Gender (boys versus girls); 2. Locality (urban versus rural); 3. Medium of Instruction (English medium versus Telugu medium); and 4. Management of the school (government versus private).

The sample for the study consists of 200 eighth class students of Nellore district. Equal weightage was given to gender (boys and girls), locality (urban and rural), medium (English and Telugu), and management (government and private).

The standardised tool "Non-Verbal Test of Creative Thinking" constructed by Beqer Mehdi was used to measure the creative thinking of secondary school students.

The collected data was analysed by employing statistical techniques like Mean, Standard Deviation and t-test.

CONCLUSIONS AND DISCUSSION

The following conclusions were drawn from the present study on "A Study of Creative Thinking of Secondary School Students". The conclusions are analysed hereunder in order to utilise them for enhancing the creative thinking of secondary school students.

1. The secondary school students are holding a high level of creative thinking.

It is very nice to observe that the secondary school students are with a high creative thinking capacity.

The secondary school students should enhance their creative thinking to other higher levels by the following strategies of promotion/development of creative thinking as suggested by various eminent psychologists.

The students should use their capacities to enhance their academic achievement, which can help them in becoming different kinds of successful professionals.

The teachers should also utilise this creative thinking in promoting various skills and abilities of students to help them settle well in academic and vocational worlds.

2. Both boys and girls of secondary schools are with high creative thinking, but there is a significant difference in the level of creative thinking of them as boys are holding high creative thinking ability than girls.

Sharma, M. (1977) found that males were superior in creativity to females. Sharma, K. (1982) found that boys were more creative as compared to girls. Kundu, D. (1984) found that males had higher scores on originality than females. Trimurthry, D. (1987) found that boys were better than the girls in both verbal, non-verbal of C.T.A. Bhogayata, C.K. (1986) found that boys were more creative than girls. Bindal, V.R. (1984) found that there was a significant relationship between verbal and non-verbal creativity for males and females. Sharma, S.C. (1979) found that males were significant by superior to females on figural originality and no significant difference was found in case of composite figural creativity. Asha, C.B. (1980) found a positive significant relationship between creativity and achievement scores of male as well as female students. Awasthy, M. (1979) found that boys scored significantly higher than girls in verbal originality and verbal total creativity. Dharmangadan, B. (1981) found that male students scored significantly higher than females in all measures of verbal and figural creativity.

Rawat, M.S. and Garg, M.K. (1977) found that girls scored significantly higher than boys on the test of creativity. Awasthy, M. (1979) found that there was no significant difference among boys and girls in verbal fluency. Chaudary, G.G. (1983) found no significant difference between the mean creativity thinking scores of male and female children of rural and urban areas. Gupta, P.K. (1985) found no significant relationship between verbal and non-verbal creativity for males and females.

Phatak (1962), Pogue (1964), Jackson (1968), Simpkins and Eisenman (1968), Burns (1969), Kaltsounis (1971), Philips and Torrance (1971), Kloss (1972), Thamma Pradeep (1976), Dutt, Bountra and Sabhrawal (1977) found no sex differences on creativity. Olshin (1965), Raina (1971), Gakhar (1974), Lal (1977), Rasool (1977), Gupta (1979), Harnek, Kaile and Sekhar (1988) found no relationship between creativity and sex. Singh (1981) observed that sex did not seem to have any significant differential effect. Sharma (1981), Pandey (1980), Thorat (1977), Vohra (1975), Raina (1971) and Singh (1978) found no significant effect between males and females on creativity.

The difference in the present study may be due to the facilities accorded to boys, social mores and norms of the society, exposure of boys to various phenomena of the world etc.

The girl students should do well in creative thinking by participating in various creative activities and by utilising different strategies that promote creative thinking.

Both the boys and girls should also try to enhance their creative thinking status through various strategies of promoting creative thinking.

3. **There is a significant difference in the level of creative thinking of urban and rural students, though both of them are possessing a high creative thinking ability. Urban school students are more creative thinkers than rural school students.**

Singh, G. (1985) found that the mean scores of urban students were higher than those of rural students. Sharma (1972) found that there was a significant difference in the creativity score of urban and rural students. Passi (1971) observed that urban students were significantly more creative than rural students. Singh (1979) found that urban residential backgrounds were more conducive for creativity than rural residential backgrounds. Singh (1977), Singh (1978) and Srivastava (1978) also reported the superiority of urban students over rural students in creativity. Dharmangadan (1981) stated that urban students scored significantly higher than rural students on flexibility and originality measures of verbal and figural creativity. According to Agarwal and Gupta (1982), locality plays a significant role in developing creative potential among the students.

Sharma (1971, 1972 and 1974) reported that rural students were significantly more creative than urban students. Sehgal (1978) also reported similar results.

Singh (1981), Joshi (1982) and Chandrakant (1987) found that there was no significant difference in the creativity of urban and rural students. Jayaswal (1977) reported no significant difference between the teacher trainees from urban and rural areas.

The urban school students might have been holding more creative thinking ability than their counter parts due to their expose to conducive educational atmosphere both in school and at home, time devoted for educational exercises, facilities available, quality in teaching and learning activities, etc., as these differ significantly in either of the schools.

Urban as well as rural school students move further in the areas of creative thinking so that they do well in all endeavours of their lives.

4. **There is a significant difference in the level of creative thinking of English medium and Telugu medium students, though both of them posses high thinking ability. English medium school students are more creative than Telugu medium school students.**

Vohra, I.N. (1975) found that English medium students were more fluent than the Gujarati medium students.

It is known to the public that the English medium schools, because of their financial position, provide excellent amenities to its clientele, which help in promoting better creative thinking capacities. Besides this, the parents, mostly belonging to elite and or rich families, contribute their best in promoting creative thinking.

All these students, irrespective of their socio-economic backgrounds at homes and academic atmosphere in the schools should become very high creative thinkers through various ways and means to meet the challenges of the day as well as future.

5. **The government and private school students are having high cre·tive thinking ability, but there is a significant difference in the level of creative thinking between them, as private school students are holding more creative thinking ability than their counterparts.**

Gupta, A.K. (1978) found that the students of private schools scored significantly higher than the students of government schools in different dimensions of verbal and non-verbal creativity.

The private schools are popular for their infrastructural and instructional facilities that cover furnished accommodation, good library, equipped laboratories, committed teachers, advanced instructional strategies, etc., which contribute for better creative thinking when compared to the government schools.

The administrators of government should also try to compete with private schools with regard to infrastructural and instructional facilities so that the government school students prosper to the core in the area of creative thinking.

In any way, both private and government school students should develop more creative thinking ability than the existing level.

6. Even both urban secondary school boys and girls hold a high creative thinking ability, there is a significant difference in the level of creative thinking of urban girls and boys. Urban school boys are with high creative thinking ability than their counterparts.

As the urban boys and girls are holding a high level of creative thinking, though with a significant difference between them, they should improve it to the core by following techniques of creative thinking development with the strong support of parents, teachers and society.

7. Though rural school boys are with high creative thinking capacity and rural school girls are just crossed low level creative thinking to high level of creative thinking, there is a significant difference in the level of creative thinking of rural girls and boys.

Both of the sub-samples rural boys and girls should strive better to reach very high level of creative thinking. The parents should provide conducive facilities at home, the teachers should encourage at school and the administrators should create opportunities everywhere for the promotion of creative thinking to rural school boys and girls.

8. **Even both urban English medium and Telugu medium secondary school students hold a high level of creative thinking capacity, there is a significant difference in the level of creative thinking between them. English medium students are superior to Telugu medium students in creative thinking.**

The urban school students, irrespective of their medium of instruction, should reach the highest range of creative thinking by following suitable strategies and by grabbing available opportunities.

9. **There is a significant difference in the level of creative thinking of rural English medium and Telugu medium school students, as former students are superior in creative thinking than the later. The rural English medium school students are with high creative thinking capacity and the rural Telugu medium school students are with low creative thinking ability.**

Both the sub-samples should strive hard to achieve a very high level of creative thinking, particularly the rural Telugu medium school students should do more than their counterparts to reach the said goal. The parents, the teachers and the authorities should do their best to achieve the affixed mark.

10. **The rural Telugu medium school boys and girls are holding a high level of creative thinking, but there is a significant difference in the level of creative thinking between them. Boys are holding more creative thinking capacity than their counterparts.**

The people who are concerned to promote the level of creative thinking in rural Telugu medium secondary school boys and girls should do their best in all walks of life in order to achieve the aim of enhancing the level of creative thinking in rural Telugu medium school students, who mostly come from the traditional vocational families with low economic status.

11. There is a significant difference in the level of creative thinking of rural English medium school boys and girls. Boys of these schools are with high creative thinking ability and girls of these schools are holding bow creative thinking capacity.

Whatever the level of creative thinking of rural English medium school boys and girls may be, the concerned parties should help these students enhance their level of creative thinking until they reach the pinnacle.

12. There is a significant difference in the level of creative thinking of urban Telugu medium school boys and girls. Boys are superior with a high level of creative thinking than girls, who are possessive, a low level of creative thinking.

When compared to urban English medium school students, the urban Telugu medium school students are with a little bit less level of creative thinking, may be due to the facilities available at school and home are different in both the cases.

The students of this category need to improve their level of creative thinking through the practices that promote it.

13. Though urban English medium school students are superior in creative thinking than their counterparts, there is a significant difference in the level of creative thinking of these students. Both of them are with high creative thinking capacity.

The urban English medium school boys and girls may enhance their level of creative thinking with a commitment for that through vigorous activities that enhance the level of creative thinking. The home, school and society should also contribute their might to help this mighty cause.

In conclusion, the secondary school students are holding a high level of creative thinking, English medium students, private school students and secondary school boys are possessing higher level of creative thinking than their counterparts.

SUGGESTIONS FOR FURTHER RESEARCH

In the present study an attempt was made to assess the creative thinking of secondary school students.

1. The study was limited to only children of eighth class students of secondary schools. Indepth studies taking all age groups starting from primary through college to university level may be conducted to trace out the level of creative thinking at each level of education.

2. The study was limited to English and Telugu medium only. A comprehensive investigation between and among different languages and cultures may be worthwhile for investigation with regard to creative thinking.

3. The study was limited to government and private managements. Investigations are possible to identify the level of creative thinking of students of different managements like zilla parishad schools, municipal schools, aided schools, and central government schools.

4. Studies may be taken up by taking the other variables like SES, birth order and other variables, which were not studied in this study.

BIBLIOGRAPHY

Adcock, C.J. and Martin, W.A. (1971). *Flexibility and Creativity.* Journal of General Psychology, 85, 71-76.

Arasteh, J.D. (1968). *Creativity and Related Processes in the Young Child.* A Review of the Literature Journal of Genetic Psychology, 112, 77-108.

Arnold, J.E.(1962). Useful Creative Techniques, (In) Parnes, S.J. and Hrding, H.F. (Eds) *A Source Book for Creative Thinking.* New York: Charles Serifner's Sons. 251-268.

Awasthy, M. (1979). *A Study of Creativity Intelligence, Scholastic Achievement and the Factors of Socio-economic Status.* Unpublished M.Ed., Dissertation, Indore University, Indore.

Agarwal, S.C. and Gupta, S.P. (1982). *A Study of Biographical Attributes of High and Low Creative Students Teachers Indian Education.* 12, 8.

Ahmed, S. (1980) *Effect of Socio-cultural Disadvantage on Creative Thinking.* Journal of Psychological Researches, 24, 2, 96-106.

Bennett, S.N. (1973). *Divergent Thinking Abilities—A Validation Study.* British Journal of Educational Psychology Today, 43, 1-7.

Bharadwaj, R. and Sharma, A.D. (1986). *Intelligence, Sex and Age as Correlates of the Components of Creativity.* Asian Journal of Psychology and Education, 16, 3, 41-44.

Bhavnani, R. and Hurr, C. (1972). *Divergent Thinking in Boys and Girls.* Journal of Child Psychology and Psychiatry.

Bishop, D.W. and Chace, C.A. (1971). *Parental Conceptual System, Home Play Environment and Potential Creativity in Children.* Journal of Experimental Child Psychology, 12, 318-338.

Bllom, B.S. (Ed) (1958). *Some Effects of Cultural, Social and Educational Conditions on Creativity* (In) Calvin, W. Taylor (Ed). The Second (1957) Conference on the Identification of Creative Scientific Talent, University of Utah Press, 55-65.

Burns, M.J. (1969). Selected Characteristics of Children's Individual Tests of Creativity. Dissertation Abstracts International, 30, 5, 1859 A.

Burgess, W.V. (1971). *The Analysis of Teacher Creativity, Pupil Age and Pupil Sex as Sources of Variation Among Elementary Pupil's Performance on Pre and Post Tests of Creative Thinking.* Dissertation Abstracts International, 32, 2, 747.

Brodley, F.K. (1976). *The Effect of Frustration on the Figural Creativity Thinking of 5th Grade Students.* Journal of Experimental Education, 44, 3, 20-23.

Badrinath, S. and Satya Narayana, S.B. (1979) *Correlates of Creative Thinking of High School Students.* Creativity News Letter, 7-8, 2 & 1, 16-23.

Cacha, F.B. (1971). *A Study of Creative Thinking Abilities of Personality Factors and Peer Nominations of Fifth Grade Children.* Dissertation Abstracts International, 32, 3, 1329A.

Child, D. and Croucher, A. (1977). *A Divergent Thinking and Ability: Is There a Threshold.* Educational Studies, 3, 101-110.

Chandrankant, Bhogayata, (1987). *The Effect of Birth Order, Sex and Urban-rural Dimensions of Culture and Creativity of Secondary School Students.* Journal of Education and Psychology, 44, 4, 212-216.

Cohen, S. and Oden, S. (1974). *An Examination of Creativity and Locus of Control in Children*. Journal of Genetic Psychology, 124, 179-185.

Cottle, T.J. (1973). *A Simple Change in Creativity*. Journal of Creative Behaviour, 7, 161-164.

Crutchfield, R.S. (1967). *Instructing the Individual in Creative Thinking (In) Ross, L. Mooney and Taher, A. Razik (Eds) Explorations in Creativity*. New York: Harper and Row, 196-205.

Dexie, F. (1985). Test of Creative Thinking Potentials, Academic Achievement, 7th-12th Grades. Information of Psychological Sciences, 2, 20-25.

Doppett (1964). *What is Creativity? III. Definitions of Creativity*. New York: Transactions, Academy of Sciences, 26, 788-793.

Drevhahal, J.E. (1956). *Factors of Importance for Creativity*. Journal of Clinical Psychology, 12, 21-26.

Dharmagandan, B.C.(1976). *Creativity in School Children: An Analytical Study*. Unpublished Ph.D. Thesis, University of Kerala, Trivandrum.

Dharmagandan, B.C. (1976). *Creativity in Relation to Sex, Age and Locality*. Psychological Studies, 26, 1, 28-33.

Eisenman, Russel (1988). *Creativity Birth Order and Risk Taking*. Buttetin of Psychonomic Society.

Elizabeth, B. Hurlock (1997). *Child Development*. New Delhi: Tata McGraw-Hill (Sixth Edition).

Foster, J. (1971). *Creativity and the Teacher*. London: Macmillan Education Ltd.

Foster, J. (1973). *Creativity*. Educational Research, 15, 217-220.

Flag, Dexie (1985). *Test of Creative Thinking Potentials, Academic Achievement, 7th-12th Graders*. Information of Psychological Sciences, 2, 20-25.

Getzels, J.W. (1959). *The Highly Intelligent and the Highly Creative Adolescent*. Research Findings, in Taylor, C.W. (Ed.), Salt Lake City: University of Utah Press, 46-57.

Greenancre, P. (1959). *Play in Relation to Creative Imagination.* Psychoanalytic Study of the Child, 14, 61-80.

Golamn, S.E. (1961). *Psychological Study of Creativity.* Psychological Bulletin, 60, 548-565.

Guilford, J.P. (1961). *Creative Thinking Abilities of Ninth-Grade Students.* Paper Presented at Annual Meeting of American Educational Research Association, Chicago.

Guilford and Hoepfner, R. (1966). *Creative Potential as Related to Measures of IQ and Verbal Comprehension.* Indian Journal of Psychology, 41,7-16.

Gakhar, S. (1974). *Creativity in Relation to Age and Sex.* Journal of Education and Psychology, 32, 3.

Gagneja, S.L. (1972). *A Study of Creativity in Ninth Class Students in Relation to Sex, Residential Background, Academic Achievement and Parental Occupation.* Master's Dissertation, Punjab University.

Harnek, S., Kaile Gurusagar, Sadhu and Manjit, K., Sekhon (1988). *Creativity in Relation of Sex and Birth Order.* The Educational Review, XCIV, 11, 195-197.

Hallman, R.J. (1963). *The Necessary and Sufficient Conditions of Creativity.* Journal of Humanistic Psychology, 3-1.

Hussain, M.G. (1974). *Creativity and Sex Differences.* Psychological Studies, 19, 2, 127-129.

Hatchinson, W.L. (1967). *Creative and Productive Thinking in the Classroom.* Journal of Creative Behaviour, 1, 4, 419-427.

Jarial, Gurpal Singh, (1979). *Verbal Creative Thinking Among the Students with Different Socio-economic Status Backgrounds and Birth Orders.* Psycho Lingua, 9, 2, 85-90.

Jarial, Gurpal Singh, (1981). *Effect of Birth Order Upon Creative Thinking Abilities Among Adolescents.* Psychological Studies, 1981 (In Press).

Jayaswal, V.K. (1977). *A Study of Creativity in Relation to Anxiety in Male and Female Teacher Trainees.* Doctoral Thesis, Gorakhpur University.

Jha, S.K. (1978) (In) Passi, B.K. (1982). *Creativity in Education*. Agra: National Psychological Corporation.

Jha, S.K. (1978) (In) Passi, B.K. (1978). *An Analysis of Certain Dimensions of Creativity*. Bombay: Himalaya Publishing House.

Kloss, M.G. (1972). *The Relation Between Adolescent Creativity and Selected Variables, Sex Adjustment, Art-science Preference, Complexity-simplicity, and Type of School*. Dissertation Abstracts International, 33, 5, 2324B.

Kogan, N. and Pankove, E. (1972). *Creative Ability Over Five-year Span*. Child Development, 43, 427-442.

Kour, R. (1978). *Personality Characteristics of High School Creative Children*. Unpublished M.A. (Ed.) Dissertation, Punjab University.

Lalithamma, M.S. (1973). *Self Concept and Creativity of Over Normal and Under Achievers Amongst Grade X Students of Baroda City*. Unpublished M.Ed., Dissertation, M.S. University, Baroda.

Mc Cloy, W. (1939). *Creative Imagination in Children and Adults*. Psychological Monographs, 51, 88-102.

Mc Dowell, M.S. and Howe, S.R. (1941). *Creative Use of Play Materials by Pre School Children*. Childhood Education, 17, 321-326.

Mac Gregor, M. and Smith, J.L. (1965). *Originality and Role Perception in Elementary and Junior High School Children*. Dissertation Abstracts, 25, 11, 6762.

Mason, J.G. (1960). *How to be a more Creative Executive*. New York: Mc Graw Hill.

Madus (1967). Quoted in Chauhan, N.S. and Tiwari. *Manual of Creativity Test*. Agra: Agra Psychological Research Cell.

Mehdi, B. (1973). *Manual: Verbal Test of Creative Thinking*. Aligrah: Mrs. Qumar Fatima.

Nair, M. (1976). *Personality Characteristics of Creative High School Pupils*. Master's Thesis, Kerala University, Trivandrum.

Newell, A. (1962) and Others. *The Process of Creative Thinking (In) Graber, H.E. et al., (Eds.) Contemporary Approaches to Creative Thinking*. Altherton Press, 63-119.

Ogilvie, E. (1974). *Creativity and Curriculum Structure*. Educational Research, 16, 126-132.

Olton, R.M. (1969). *The Development of Productive Thinking Skills in Fifth Grade Children. Wisconsin Research and Development Centre for Cognitive Learning*. University of Wisconsin, Madison.

Olshin, G.M. (1965). *The Relationship Along Selected Subjected Variables and Levels of Creativity*. Exceptional Children. 31, 588-589.

Ogletree, E.J.A. (1968). *Cross-cultural Exploratory Study of the Creativeness of Steiner and State School Pupils in England*. Scotland and Germany, Dissertation Abstracts, 29, 2, 516A.

Ogletree, E.J.A. (1971). *A Cross-cultural Examination of the Creative Thinking Ability of Public and Private School Pupils in England*. Scotland and Germany. Journal of Social Psychology, 83, 301-302.

Osborn (1957). *Creative Imagination*. New York: Charles Scribner Sons, 3rd Ed.

Pandey, R.C. and Pandy, R.N. (1984). *A Study of Creativity in Relation to Sex of High School Students*. Indian Psychological Review, 26, 2, 53-57.

Pandit, R. (1972). *An Exploratory Study of Creativity and Its Relationship with Intelligence and Achievement in School Subjects at Higher Secondary Stages*. Doctoral Thesis, Punjab University.

Patrick, Catherine. (1955). *What is Creative Thinking?* New York: Philosophical Library.

Parnes, S.J. (1966). *Work Book for Creative Problem Solving Institutes and Courses*. Buffalo: Creative Education Foundation.

Passi, B.K. (1972). *An Exploratory Study of Creativity and Its Relationship with Intelligence and Achievement in School Subjects at Higher Secondary Stages*. Doctoral Thesis, Punjab University.

Passi, B.K. (1979). *Passi Test of Creativity (Verbal and Non-verbal)*. Agra: National Psychological Corporation.

Patel, A.S. (1978). *An Enquiry in to the Relation of Creativity to Intellectual Giftedness*. Indian Journal of Psychology, 53, 3, 140-144.

Peet, Harruet, E. (1960). *The Creative Individual: A study of New Perspectives in American Education.* New York: The Ronald Press Company.

Phatak (1962). *Experimental Study of Creativity and Intelligence and School Achievements.* Psychological Studies, 7, 1-9.

Philips, V.K. and Torrance, E.P. (1971). *Divergent Thinking Remote Associations and Concept Attainment Strategies.* Journal of Psychology, 77, 223-228.

Pogue, B.C. (1964). *A Study to Determine Whether or not there is a Relationship Between Creativity and Self Image.* Doctoral Dissertation, Bale State University.

Raina, M.K. (1969). *A Study of Sex Differences in Creativity in India.* Journal of Creative Behaviour, 3, 111-114.

Raina, M.K. (1970). *A Study of Creative Teachers.* Psychological Studies, 15, 1 & 2, 28-33.

Raina, M.K. (1971). *Verbal and Non-vernal Creative Thinking Ability: A Study in Sex Differences.* Journal of Education and Psychology, 29, 3, 175-179.

Ramey, C.T. and Piper, V. (1974). *Creativity in Open and Traditional Classrooms.* Child Development, 45, 557-560.

Roger, C.R. (1962) Towards a Theory of Creativity (In) Parnes, S.J. and Harding, H.F. (Eds.). *A Source Book for Creative Thinking.* 63-2, New York: Scribner.

Roger, C.R. (1969) Towards a Theory of Creativity (In) Anderson, H.D. (Ed.,) *Creativity and Its Cultivation.* New York, 70: Harper and Row.

Razik, T.M.A. *An Investigation of Creative Thinking Among College Students.* Dissertation Abstracts, 24, 7, 2775.

Ruth, Jen-Evik and Birren James, E. (1985). *Creativity in Adulthood and Old Age, Relations to Intelligence, Sex and Mode of Testing.* International Journal of Behavioural Development, 8,1, 99-107.

Rawat, M.S. and Garg, M.K. (1977). *A Study of Creativity and Level of Aspiration of High School Students.* Indian Psychological Review, 14, 2, 51-53.

Rasool, G. (1977). *A Study of Divergent Thinking of School Going Children*. Creativity Newsletter, 6, 3, 23-26.

Rawat, M.S. and Agarwal, S. (1977). *A Study of Creative Thinking with Reference to Intelligence, Age, Sex, Communities and Income Group*. Indian Psychological Review, 14, 2, 36-40.

Syama Thirumurthy (1987). *Creative Thinking Ability as a Function of Sex Intelligence and Study Habits*. Journal of Education and Psychology, 45, 1, 51, 56.

Sansanwal, D.N. and Jarial, Gurupal Singh (1979). *Personality Differences Among High and Low Creative Teacher Trainees*. Journal of the Institute of Educational Research. 3, 3, 24-26.

Sansanwal, D.N. and Jarial, Gurupal Singh (1980). *Creativity and Age*. Creativity Newsletters. (In Press)

Sansanwal, D.N. and Jarial, Gurupal Singh, 1981 (In) Passi B.K. (1982). *Creativity in Education*. Agra: National Psychological Corporation.

Shukla, Prakash Chandra (1982). *A Study of Creativity in Relation to Sex, Locality and School Subjects*. Indian Educational Review, 17,2, 128-132.

Seetharam, R. and Vedanayagam, E.G. (1979). *Creativity and Socio-economic Status*. Journal of the Institute of Educational Research, 3, 4, 35-37.

Sharma, A.K. (1980). *Creativity and Its Components as Affected by Socio-economic Status and Personality Experiments in Education*. 8, 7, 129-133.

Straus, J.H. and Straus. M.A. (1968). *Family Roles and Sex Differences in Creativity in Children in Bombay and Minneapolis*. Journal of Marriage and Family, 30, 1, 46-53.

Singh, D. (1978). *A Study of the Personality Correlates of Creativity Children (15+) Studying Science Subjects*. Doctoral Thesis, Bhopal University.

Sivarathnam Reddy, M. (1994). *A Study of Creativity of Students at +2 Level in Relation to Some Variables*. Ph.D., Thesis, S.V. University, Tirupati.

Sudhakar Reddy, P. (1990). *A Investigation into the Creativity of Adolescent Boys and Girls.* Ph.D., Thesis, S.V. University, Tirupati.

Raja Sekhar Reddy, T. (2002). *Creativity: Its Correlates Certain Personal, Social and Psychological Variables of Student Teachers of DIETs.* Ph.D., Thesis, S.V. University, Tiruapti.

Taylor, C.W. (1964). *Creativity: Progress and Potential.* New York: McGraw Hill.

Thamma Pratap, V. (1976). *A Comparative Study of Creativity of Indian Students (Baroda) and Thai Students (Nakornsawan) of Grade IX.* Unpublished M.Ed., Dissertation, M.S. University, Baroda.

Thorndike, R.L. (1963). *Some Methodological Issues in Study of Creativity (In) Gardner, E.F. (Ed) Proceedings of 1962 Invitational Conference on Testing Problems.* Princeton: Educational Testing Service.

Thurston, L.L. (1952). *Creative Talent, in L.L. Thurston (Ed.) Application Psychology.* New York: Harper & Brothers.

Trow Bridge, N. (1966). *Research on Creativity (In) Patel. A.S. and Shah G.B. (Eds.) Education of Backward and the Gifted Children.* Centre for Advanced study in Education. Baroda.

Trivedi, R.C. (1969). *To Establish the Reliability and Validity of the Tests of Creativity.* Unpublished M.Ed., Dissertation, Punjab University.

Torrance, E.P. (1964). *Education and Creativity (In) Taylor, C.W. (Ed.) Creativity: Progress and Potential.* New York: McGraw Hill.

Torrance, E.P. (1964). *The Minnesota Studies of Creative Thinking (In) Taylor, C.W. (Ed.) Widening Horizons in Creativity.* New York: John Wiley & Sons, Inc.

Torrance, E.P. (1968). *Examples and Rationale of Tests for Assessing Creative Abilities.* Journal of Creative Behaviour, 2, 165-178.

Torrance, E.P. (1972). *Can We Teach Children to Think Creatively?* Journal of Creative Behaviour.16, 2.

Torrance, E.P, et al., (19600. *Minnesota Studies of Creative Thinking in the Early School Years.* Research Memorandum BERR-60-1, University of Minnesota, Minneapolis, Minnesota, 30-31.

Torrance, E.P. (1960). *Exploration in Creative Thinking Education*. 18, 216-220.

Torrance, E.P. and his Associates (1960). *Exploration in Creative Thinking in the Early School Years. XI Changing Reactions of Girls in Grades Four Through Six to Tasks Requiring Creative Scientific Thinking*. Research Memorandum No. 60-12. University of Minnesota, Bureau of Educational Research, Minneapolis, Minnesota.

Torrance, E.P. (1961). *Factors Affecting Creative Thinking in Children*. An Interim Research Report. Merrill Palmer Quarterly, 7, 171-180.

Torrance, E.P. (1963). *Changing Reactions of Pre-adolescent Girls to Take Requiring Creative Scientific Thinking*. Journal of Genetic Psychology, 102, 217-223.

Torrance, E.P. (1964). *Education and Creativity (In) Taylor C.W. (Ed.) Creativity Progress and Potential*. 50-128, New York: McGraw Hills.

Torrance, E.P. and Gowan, (1963) (In) Passi, B.K. Passi *Tests of Creativity (Verbal and Non-verbal)*. Agra: National Psychological Corporation.

Torrance, E.P. (1988). *Achievement of Students Under Detention and Non-detection Systems*. Indian Educational Review, 41-45.

Tumin, M. (1953). *Obstacles to Creativity*. ETC, 11, 261-271.

Verma, L.K. (1980). *A Study of Locus of Control of High and Low Creative School Students at Different Levels of Socio-economic Status*. Journal of Education and Psychology, 38, 2, 99-104.

Verma, R.S. (1973). *A Factor Analytic Study of Divergent Thinking in Relation to Certain Personality Dimensions of Higher Secondary School Adolescents*. Doctoral Thesis, Aligarh Muslim University.

Vernon, P.E. (1964). *Creativity and Intelligence*. Educational Research, 6, 163-176.

Vohara, I.N. (1975). *A Study of Non-verbal Creativity in Relation to Socio-economic Status, Age, Medium of Instruction and Personality Characteristics Amongst the Pupils of English and Gujarati Medium of "Bazm-E-Hidayat" Primary School from Baroda City*. Unpublished M.Ed. Dissertation, M.S. University.

Walker, P.C. (1969). *A Study of Creativity Among Mexican School Children*. Doctoral Dissertation, University of Georgia.

Welch, L. (1946). *Recombination of Ideas in Creative Thinking*. Journal of Applied Psychology, 30, 638-643.

Wilson, R.G. and Lewis, D.J. (1954). *A Factor Analytical Study of Creative Thinking Abilities*. Psychometrics, 19, 297-311.

Wodtke, K.H. (1964). *Some Data on the Reliability and Validity of Creativity Tests at the Elementary School Level*. Educational and Psychological Measurement, 24, 2, 339-408.

Yamamoto, K. (1960). *The Role of Creative Thinking and Intelligence in High School Achievement*. Research Memorandum, BER-60-10. Bureau of Educational Research, College of Education, University of Minnesota, 1-245.

Zargar, A.H. and Neelam Dhar (1988). *Creativity and Socio-economic Status: A Study*. The Educational Review, XCIV, 29-31.

Zirbes, Laura (1959). *Spurs of Creative Teaching*. New York: G.P. Putnam's Sons.

Additional References

Bhaskara Rao, Digumarti (1994). *Scientific Aptitude*. New Delhi: Ashish Publishing House. ISBN 81-7024-658-X.

Bhaskara Rao, Digumarti (1995). *Animal Kingdom*. New Delhi: Discovery Publishing House. ISBN 81-7141-274-2.

Bhaskara Rao, Digumarti (1995). *Batracology*. New Delhi: Discovery Publishing House. ISBN 81-7141-279-3.

Bhaskara Rao, Digumarti (1997). *Scientific Attitude*. New Delhi: Discovery Publishing House. ISBN 81-7141-381-1.

Bhaskara Rao, Digumarti (1996). *Scientific Attitude vis-à-vis Scientific Aptitude*. New Delhi: Discovery Publishing House. ISBN 81-7141-308-0.

Bhaskara Rao, Digumarti (2004). *Scientific Attitude, Scientific Aptitude and Achievement*. New Delhi: Discovery Publishing House. ISBN 81-7141-781-7.

Bhaskara Rao, Digumarti (2004). *Educational Administration*. New Delhi: Discovery Publishing House. ISBN 81-7141-842-2.

Bhaskara Rao, Digumarti (2004). *Issues in School Education*. New Delhi: Discovery Publishing House. ISBN 81-8356-025-3.

Bhaskara Rao, Digumarti, Editor (1996). *Encyclopaedia of Education For All*, 5 Volumes. New Delhi: APH Publishing Corporation. ISBN 81-7024-759-4 (set).

Vol. I *Education For All: The World Conference*. ISBN 81-7024-760-8.

Vol. II *Education For All: The EPA-9 Summit*. ISBN 81-7024-761-6.

Vol. III *Education For All: Quality Education For All*. ISBN 81-7024-762-6.

Vol. IV *Education For All: Planning and Monitoring*. ISBN 81-7024-763-4.

Vol. V *Education For All: The Indian Scenario*. ISBN 81-7024-764-0.

Bhaskara Rao, Digumarti, Editor (1996). *National Policy on Education*, 2 Volumes. New Delhi: Anmol Publications Pvt. Ltd. ISBN 81-7488-323-1.

Bhaskara Rao, Digumarti, Editor (1996). *Global Perceptions on Peace Education*, 3 Volumes. New Delhi: Discovery Publishing House. ISBN 81-7141-319-6.

Bhaskara Rao, Digumarti, Editor (1997). *Education for the 21st Century*. New Delhi: Discovery Publishing House. ISBN 81-7141-389-7.

Bhaskara Rao, Digumarti, Editor (1997). *Reflections on Scientific Attitude*. New Delhi: Discovery Publishing House. ISBN 81-7141-319-6.

Bhaskara Rao, Digumarti, Editor (1997). *Success Story of a Primary Education Project*. New Delhi: APH Publishing Corporation. ISBN 81-7024-850-7.

Bhaskara Rao, Digumarti, Editor (1997). *World Food Summit*. New Delhi: Discovery Publishing House. ISBN 81-7141-386-2.

Bhaskara Rao, Digumarti, Editor (1997). *Care the Child*, 2 Volumes. New Delhi: Discovery Publishing House. ISBN 81-7141-394-3.

Bhaskara Rao, Digumarti, Editor (1998). *Earth Summit*, 2 Volumes. New Delhi: Discovery Publishing House. ISBN 81-7141-435-4.

Bhaskara Rao, Digumarti, Editor (1998). *Adolescence Education*. New Delhi: Discovery Publishing House. ISBN 81-7141-432-X.

Bhaskara Rao, Digumarti, Editor (1998). *Community and School Nutrition Education*. New Delhi: Discovery Publishing House. ISBN 81-7141-435-4.

Bhaskara Rao, Digumarti, Editor (1998). *District Primary Education Programme*. New Delhi: Discovery Publishing House. ISBN 81-7141-396-X.

Bhaskara Rao, Digumarti, Editor (1998). *National Policy on Education: Towards an Enlightened and Humane Society*. New Delhi: Discovery Publishing House. ISBN 81-7141-426-5.

Bhaskara Rao, Digumarti, Editor (1998). *Reforming School Education*. New Delhi: Discovery Publishing House. ISBN 81-7141-403-6.

Bhaskara Rao, Digumarti, Editor (1998). *Teacher Education in India*. New Delhi: Discovery Publishing House. ISBN 81-7141-406-0.

Bhaskara Rao, Digumarti, Editor (1998). *World Summit for Social Development*. New Delhi: Discovery Publishing House. ISBN 81-7141-420-6.

Bhaskara Rao, Digumarti, Editor (1999). *International Encyclopaedia of AIDS*, 11 Volumes. New Delhi: Discovery Publishing House. ISBN 81-7141-522-6 (set).

Vol. 1 *Introduction to HIV/AIDS*. ISBN 81-7141-523-7.

Vol. 2 *HIV/AIDS – Issues and Challenges*, 2 Parts. ISBN 81-7141-524-5.

Vol. 3 *HIV/AIDS—Socio-economic Realities*. ISBN 81-7141-524-3.

Vol. 4 *HIV/AIDS—Law Ethics and Human Rights*, 2 Parts. ISBN 81-7141-526-1.

Vol. 5 *AIDS and NGOs*. ISBN 81-7141-527-X.

Vol. 6 *AIDS and Home Care*. ISBN 81-7141-528-8.

Vol. 7 *STD Case Management*. ISBN 81-7141-529-6.

Vol. 8 *HIV/AIDS Prevention and Care—Teaching Modules for Nurses and Midwives*. ISBN 81-7141-530-X.

Vol. 9 *HIV Prevention Education for Educational Institutions*. ISBN 81-7141-531-8.

Vol. 10 *Instructional Modules for AIDS Education*. ISBN 81-7141-532-6.

Vol. 11 *School Health Education to Prevent AIDS and STD—A Package for Curriculum Planners*. ISBN 81-7141-533-4.

Bhaskara Rao, Digumarti, Editor (2000). *International Encyclopaedia of Human Rights*, 7 Volumes in 13 Parts. New Delhi: Discovery Publishing House. ISBN 81-7141-567-9 (set).

Vol. 1 *International Instruments of Human Rights*, 2 Parts. ISBN 81-7141-569-4.

Vol. 2 *Regional Instruments of Human Rights*. ISBN 81-7141-604-7.

Vol. 3 *Human Rights and the United Nations*, 2 parts. ISBN 81-7141-605-5.

Vol. 4 *Fact Files of Human Rights*, 3 Parts. ISBN 81-7141-606-3.

Vol. 5 *Study Stories of Human Rights*, 3 Parts. ISBN 81-7141-607-3.

Vol. 6 *International Meetings on Human Rights*, 2 Parts. ISBN 81-7141-608-X.

Vol. 7 *Professional Training in Human Rights*. ISBN 81-7141-609-8.

Bhaskara Rao, Digumarti, Editor (2000). *International Encyclopaedia of Science and Technology Education*, 11 Volumes. New Delhi: Discovery Publishing House. ISBN 81-7141-548-2 (set).

Vol. 1 *Science and Technology Education*. ISBN 81-7141-568-7.

Vol. 2 *Science Education in Developing Countries*. ISBN 81-7141-569-9.

Vol. 3 *Organisational Structure of Science*. ISBN 81-7141-570-9.

Vol. 4 *Science Education in Asia and the Pacific*. ISBN 81-7141-571-7.

Vol. 5 *Science and Technology Education For All*. ISBN 81-7141-572-5.

Vol. 6 *Values, Ethics, Talent and Girls in Science and Technology Education*. ISBN 81-7141-573-3.

Vol. 7 *Popularisation of Science and Technology Education*. ISBN 81-7141-574-1.

Vol. 8 *Science, Power and Society*. ISBN 81-7141-575-X.

Vol. 9 *Information Technology*. ISBN 81-7141-576-8.

Vol. 10 *Teacher Training in Science and Technology Education*. ISBN 81-7142-577-6.

Vol. 11 *Teacher Training in Science and Technology: A Curriculum Framework*. ISBN 81-7141-578-4.

Bhaskara Rao, Digumarti, Editor (2000). *Education For All: Achieving the Goal*, 3 Volumes. New Delhi: APH Publishing Corporation. ISBN 81-7648-152-1 (set).

Vol. I *The Global Consensus*. ISBN 81-7648-155-6.

Vol. II *Mid-Decade Review Reports of Regional Seminars*. ISBN 81-7648-154-8.

Vol. III: *Issues and Trends*. ISBN 81-7648-155-6.

Bhaskara Rao, Digumarti, Editor (2001). *Nuclear Materials: Issues and Concerns*, 2 Volumes. New Delhi: Discovery Publishing House. ISBN 81-7141-611-X.

Bhaskara Rao, Digumarti, Editor (2001). *Distance Education in Different Countries*. New Delhi: APH Publishing Corporation. ISBN 81-7648-229-3.

Bhaskara Rao, Digumarti, Editor (2001). *Decentralised Management of Education: Management of Education in Panchayati Raj and Municipal Bodies*. New Delhi: Discovery Publishing House. ISBN 81-7141-617-9.

Bhaskara Rao, Digumarti, Editor (2001). *Electrochemistry for Environmental Protection*. New Delhi: Discovery Publishing House. ISBN 81-7141-619-5.

Bhaskara Rao, Digumarti, Editor (2001). *Global Educational Studies*. New Delhi: Discovery Publishing House. ISBN 81-7141-616-0.

Bhaskara Rao, Digumarti, Editor (2001). *Global Synthesis of Educational Assessment*. New Delhi: Discovery Publishing House. ISBN 81-7141-613-6.

Bhaskara Rao, Digumarti, Editor (2001). *Jomtein Decade of Education*. New Delhi: Discovery Publishing House. ISBN 81-7141-618-7.

Bhaskara Rao, Digumarti, Editor (2001). *World Conference on Education for All*. New Delhi: Discovery Publishing House. ISBN 81-7141-274-9.

Bhaskara Rao, Digumarti, Editor (2001). *World Conference on Higher Education*. New Delhi: Discovery Publishing House. ISBN 81-7141-610-1.

Bhaskara Rao, Digumarti, Editor (2001). *World Conference on Science*. New Delhi: Discovery Publishing House. ISBN 81-7141-612-8.

Bhaskara Rao, Digumarti, Editor (2003). *Inspiring Experiences in Teacher Education*. New Delhi: Discovery Publishing House. ISBN 81-7141-656-X.

Bhaskara Rao, Digumarti, Editor (2003). *International Studies in Education*, 3 Volumes. New Delhi: Discovery Publishing House. ISBN 81-7141-647-0.

Bhaskara Rao, Digumarti, Editor (2003). *Military Conversion: Impact on Science and Technology*. New Delhi: Discovery Publishing House. ISBN 81-7141-578-4.

Bhaskara Rao, Digumarti, Editor (2003). *United Nations Millennium Summit*. New Delhi: Discovery Publishing House. ISBN 81-7141-632-2.

Bhaskara Rao, Digumarti, Editor (2003). *World Assembly on Aging*. New Delhi: Discovery Publishing House. ISBN 81-7141-637-3.

Bhaskara Rao, Digumarti, Editor (2003). *World Conference on Human Rights*. New Delhi: Discovery Publishing House. ISBN 81-7141-661-6.

Bhaskara Rao, Digumarti, Editor (2003). *World Education Forum*. New Delhi: Discovery Publishing House. ISBN 81-7141-639-X.

Bhaskara Rao, Digumarti, Editor (2003). *Education, Employment and Human Resource Development*. New Delhi: Discovery Publishing House. ISBN 81-7141-681-0.

Bhaskara Rao, Digumarti, Editor (2003). *Successful Schooling*. New Delhi: Discovery Publishing House. ISBN 81-7141-677-2.

Bhaskara Rao, Digumarti, Editor (2003). *European Education and Teachers*. New Delhi: Discovery Publishing House. ISBN 81-7141-702-7.

Bhaskara Rao, Digumarti, Editor (2003). *Teachers in a Changing World*. New Delhi: Discovery Publishing House. ISBN 81-7141-694-2.

Bhaskara Rao, Digumarti, Editor (2004). *International Guidelines on Open and Distance Teacher Education*. New Delhi: Discovery Publishing House. ISBN 81-7141-777-9.

Bhaskara Rao, Digumarti, Editor (2004). *Adult Learning in the 21st Century*. New Delhi: Discovery Publishing House. ISBN 81-7141-797-3.

Bhaskara Rao, Digumarti, Editor (2004). *Educational Practices: Research and Recommendations*. New Delhi: Discovery Publishing House. ISBN 81-7141-835-X.

Bhaskara Rao, Digumarti, Editor (2004). *General Secondary Education In the 21st Century*. New Delhi: Discovery Publishing House.

Bhaskara Rao, Digumarti, Editor (2004). *International Encyclopaedia of Learning to Live Together*, 4 Volumes. New Delhi: Discovery Publishing House. ISBN 81-7141-848-1.

Vol. 1 International Conference on Learning to Live Together.

Vol. 2 Globalisation and Living Together.

Vol. 3 Curriculum for Learning to Live Together.

Vol. 4 Science Education for the Contemporary Society.

Bhaskara Rao, Digumarti, Editor (2004). *Reforming Secondary Education*. New Delhi: Discovery Publishing House. ISBN 81-7141-843-0.

Bhaskara Rao, Digumarti, Editor (2004). *Human Rights Education*. New Delhi: Discovery Publishing House. ISBN 81-7141-882-1.

Bhaskara Rao, Digumarti, Editor (2004). *United Nations Decade for Human Rights Education*. New Delhi: Discovery Publishing House. ISBN 81-7141-887-2.

Bhaskara Rao, Digumarti, Editor (2004). *Technical and Vocational Education and Training in the 21st Century*. New Delhi: Discovery Publishing House. ISBN 81-7141-984-4.

Bhaskara Rao, Digumarti, Editor (2007). *Encyclopaedia of Teacher Education*, 4 Volumes. New Delhi: Discovery Publishing House. ISBN 81-8356-306-6.

Bhaskara Rao, Digumarti, Editor (1996). *Encyclopaedia of Education For All*, 5 Volumes. New Delhi: APH Publishing Corporation. ISBN 81-7024-759-4 (set).

Bhaskara Rao, Digumarti and B.S.V. Dutt, Editors (2003). *Education: Programmes and Policies*. New Delhi: APH Publishing Corporation. ISBN 81-7648-470-9.

Bhaskara Rao, Digumarti, C.A.P. Swamy and B.S.V. Dutt (1997). *Self-Evaluation in Student Teaching*. New Delhi: Discovery Publishing House. ISBN 81-7141-374-9.

Bhaskara Rao, Digumarti and D. Naresh Kumar (2004). *School Teacher Effectiveness*. New Delhi: Discovery Publishing House. ISBN 81-7141-782-5.

Bhaskara Rao, Digumarti and D. Sridhar (2002). *Job Satisfaction of School Teachers*. New Delhi: Discovery Publishing House. ISBN 81-7141-652-7.

Bhaskara Rao, Digumarti, C. Sridevi and K. Vijaya (1995). *Achievement in Social Studies*. New Delhi: Discovery Publishing House. ISBN 81-7141-281-5.

Bhaskara Rao, Digumarti and Digumarti Pushpa Latha (1994). *Achievement in Biology*. New Delhi: Discovery Publishing House. ISBN 81-7141-264-5.

Bhaskara Rao, Digumarti and Digumarti Pushpa Latha (1995). *Achievement in English*. New Delhi: Discovery Publishing House. ISBN 81-7141-283-1.

Bhaskara Rao, Digumarti and Digumarti Pushpa Latha (1994). *Achievement in Science*. New Delhi: Discovery Publishing House. ISBN 81-7141-280-70.

Bhaskara Rao, Digumarti and Digumarti Pushpa Latha (1995). *Achievement in Mathematics*. New Delhi: Discovery Publishing House. ISBN 81-7141-278-5.

Bhaskara Rao, Digumarti and Digumarti Pushpa Latha (2004). *Education for Women*. New Delhi: Discovery Publishing House. ISBN 81-7141-873-2.

Bhaskara Rao, Digumarti, Digumarti Pushpa Latha and Digumarthi Harshitha, Editors (2001). *Biological Warfare*. New Delhi: Discovery Publishing House. ISBN 81-7141-597-0.

Bhaskara Rao, Digumarti, Digumarti Pushpa Latha and Digumarthi Harshitha, Editors (2001). *Women as Educators*. New Delhi: Discovery Publishing House. ISBN 81-7141-602-0.

Bhaskara Rao, Digumarti and Digumarthi Harshitha (2004). *Adjustment of Adolescents*. New Delhi: APH Publishing House. ISBN 81-7648-836-8.

Bhaskara Rao, Digumarti and Digumarthi Harshitha, Editors (2001). *Education in India*. New Delhi: APH Publishing House. ISBN 81-7648-207-2.

Bhaskara Rao, Digumarti and Digumarti Pushpa Latha, Editors (1998). *International Encyclopaedia of Women*, 5 Volumes. New Delhi: Discovery Publishing House. ISBN 81-7141-410-9 (set).

Vol. 1 *Status of World's Women*. ISBN 81-7141-494-X.

Vol. 2 *Women, Education and Empowerment*. ISBN 81-7141-498-1.

Vol. 3 *Women Challenges and Advancement*. ISBN 81-7141-497-4.

Vol. 4 *Women and Family Health*. ISBN 81-7141-497-4.

Vol. 5 *Women and International Action*. ISBN 81-7141-498-2.

Bhaskara Rao, Digumarti, Digumarti Pushpa Latha and Digumarthi Harshitha, Editors (2001). *Assessing Learning Achievement*. New Delhi: Discovery Publishing House. ISBN 81-7141-601-2.

Bhaskara Rao, Digumarti, Digumarti Pushpa Latha and Digumarthi Harshitha, Editors (2001). *Energy Security*. New Delhi: Discovery Publishing House. ISBN 81-7141-598-9.

Bhaskara Rao, Digumarti, Digumarthi Harshitha and K.R.S. Sambasiva Rao, Editors (1999). *Advanced Biotechnology*. New Delhi: Discovery Publishing House. ISBN 81-7141-516-4.

Bhaskara Rao, Digumarti and K.R.S. Sambasiva Rao, Editors (1996). *Current Trends in Indian Education*. New Delhi: Discovery Publishing House. ISBN 81-7141-311-0.

Bhaskara Rao, Digumarti and E. Sreekanth Babu (2004). *Educational Interests of School Students*. New Delhi: Discovery Publishing House. ISBN 81-7141-837-6.

Bhaskara Rao, Digumarti and K. Vijaya (1995). *A Text Book Evaluation*. Ambala Cantt: The Associated Publishers.

Bhaskara Rao, Digumarti and M.A. Fayaz (2004). *Problems of Primary School Drop-outs*. New Delhi: Discovery Publishing House. ISBN 81-7141-834-1.

Bhaskara Rao, Digumarti and N.V.M. Mohana Rao (2002). *Problems of Mentally Handicapped Children*. New Delhi: Discovery Publishing House. ISBN 81-7141-645-4.

Bhaskara Rao, Digumarti and S. Chandra Mohan (2002). *Sports Management*. New Delhi: APH Publishing House. ISBN 81-7648-467-9.

Bhaskara Rao, Digumarti and S.A. Khader (2004). *Problems of Private School Teachers*. New Delhi: Discovery Publishing House. ISBN 81-7141-838-4.

Bhaskara Rao, Digumarti and S.A. Khader (2004). *School Education in India*. New Delhi: Discovery Publishing House. ISBN 81-7141-849-X.

Bhaskara Rao, Digumarti and Sk. Johni Basha (2004). *Teachers' Population Education Awareness*. New Delhi: Discovery Publishing House. ISBN 81-7141-832-5.

Bhaskara Rao, Digumarti, V.V. Rao, V.V. Lakshmi and V.V. Krishna, Editors (1999). *Status and Advancement of Women*. New Delhi: APH Publishing Corporation. ISBN 81-7648-169-6.

Appala Naidu, P.Ch., Author and Digumarti Bhaskara Rao, Editor (2007). *Feedback Methods and Student Performance*. New Delhi: Discovery Publishing House. ISBN 81-8356-284-1.

Babu, P.C., Author and Digumarti Bhaskara Rao, Editor (2004). *Flowers of Wisdom*. New Delhi: Discovery Publishing House. ISBN 81-7141-695-0.

Bujji Babu, K., Author and Digumarti Bhaskara Rao, Editor (2007). *Teaching Aptitude of Primary School Teachers*. New Delhi: Sonali Publications. ISBN 81-8411-083-9.

Amala, P.A. and Anupama, P., Authors and Digumarti Bhaskara Rao, Editor (2004). *History of Education*. New Delhi: Discovery Publishing House. ISBN 81-7141-860-0.

Bhagya Lakshmi, L., Author and Digumarti Bhaskara Rao, Editor (2000). *Reading and Comprehension*. New Delhi: Discovery Publishing House. ISBN 81-7141-543-1.

Bhasha, S.A., Author and Digumarti Bhaskara Rao, Editor (2004). *Methods of Teaching Geography*. New Delhi: Discovery Publishing House. ISBN 81-7141-807-4.

Bhuvaneswara Lakshmi, Gadde, Author and Digumarti Bhaskara Rao, Editor (2000). *Attitude Towards Science*. New Delhi: Discovery Publishing House. ISBN 81-7141-541-6.

Bhuvaneswara Lakshmi, G., Author and Digumarti Bhaskara Rao, Editor (2004). *Methods of Teaching Life Science*. New Delhi: Discovery Publishing House. ISBN 81-7141-804-X.

Bhuvaneswara Lakshmi, G. and K. Subba Rao, Authors and Digumarti Bhaskara Rao, Editor (2004). *Methods of Teaching Biology*. New Delhi: Discovery Publishing House. ISBN 81-7141-914-3.

Brahmaiah, T., Author and Digumarti Bhaskara Rao, Editor (2008). *Stress of Prospective Teachers*. New Delhi: Sonali Publications.

Chary, K.V.N.B., Author and Digumarti Bhaskara Rao, Editor (2006). *Techniques of Teaching Physics*. New Delhi: Sonali Publications. ISBN 81-8411-046-4.

Chowdary, S.B.J.R. and Naga Raju, Authors and Digumarti Bhaskara Rao, Editor (2004). *Mastery of Teaching Skills*. New Delhi: Discovery Publishing House. ISBN 81-7141-861-9.

Dayakara Reddy, V. and Digumarti Bhaskara Rao, Editors (2006). *Value-Oriented Education*. New Delhi: Discovery Publishing House. ISBN 81-8356-051-2.

Devraj, T.A.S., Author and Digumarti Bhaskara Rao, Editor (1997). *Trace Analysis of Uranium and Thorium*. New Delhi: Discovery Publishing House. ISBN 81-7141-375-7.

Durga Rani, K., Author and Digumarti Bhaskara Rao, Editor (2000). *Educational Aspirations and Scientific Attitudes*. New Delhi: Discovery Publishing House. ISBN 81-7141-555-5.

Dutt, B.S.V. and Digumarti Bhaskara Rao (2001). *Empowering Primary Teachers*. New Delhi: Discovery Publishing House. ISBN 81-7141-615-2.

Dutt, B.S.V., Author and Digumarti Bhaskara Rao, Editor (2004). *Comparative Education*. New Delhi: Discovery Publishing House. ISBN 81-7141-912-7.

Ediger, Marlow and Digumarti Bhaskara Rao (1996). *Science Curriculum*. New Delhi: Discovery Publishing House. ISBN 81-7141-321-8.

Ediger, Marlow and Digumarti Bhaskara Rao (2000). *Teaching Mathematics Successfully*. New Delhi: Discovery Publishing House. ISBN 81-7141-552-0.

Ediger, Marlow and Digumarti Bhaskara Rao (2001). *Teaching Science Successfully*. New Delhi: Discovery Publishing House. ISBN 81-7141-600-4.

Ediger, Marlow and Digumarti Bhaskara Rao (2001). *Teaching Social Studies Successfully*. New Delhi: Discovery Publishing House. ISBN 81-7141-596-2.

Ediger, Marlow and Digumarti Bhaskara Rao (2002). *Philosophy and Curriculum*. New Delhi: Discovery Publishing House. ISBN 81-7141-631-4.

Ediger, Marlow and Digumarti Bhaskara Rao (2002). *Improving School Administration*. New Delhi: Discovery Publishing House. ISBN 81-7141-633-0.

Ediger, Marlow and Digumarti Bhaskara Rao (2002). *Elementary Curriculum*. New Delhi: Discovery Publishing House. ISBN 81-7141-658-6.

Ediger, Marlow and Digumarti Bhaskara Rao (2003). *Language Arts Curriculum*. New Delhi: Discovery Publishing House. ISBN 81-7141-657-8.

Ediger, Marlow and Digumarti Bhaskara Rao (2003). *Psychology and Curriculum*. New Delhi: Discovery Publishing House. ISBN 81-7141-691-8.

Ediger, Marlow and Digumarti Bhaskara Rao (2003). *Teaching Language Arts Successfully*. New Delhi: Discovery Publishing House. ISBN 81-7141-678-0.

Ediger, Marlow and Digumarti Bhaskara Rao (2003). *School Curriculum and Administration*. New Delhi: Discovery Publishing House. ISBN 81-7141-709-4.

Ediger, Marlow and Digumarti Bhaskara Rao (2003). *Teaching Mathematics in Elementary Schools*. New Delhi: Discovery Publishing House. ISBN 81-7141-687-X.

Ediger, Marlow and Digumarti Bhaskara Rao (2003). *Teaching Science in Elementary Schools*. New Delhi: Discovery Publishing House. ISBN 81-7141-698-5.

Ediger, Marlow and Digumarti Bhaskara Rao (2003). *School Curriculum and Administration*. New Delhi: Discovery Publishing House. ISBN 81-7141-709-4.

Ediger, Marlow and Digumarti Bhaskara Rao (2003). *Elementary Curriculum Improvement*. New Delhi: Discovery Publishing House. ISBN 81-7141-740-X.

Ediger, Marlow and Digumarti Bhaskara Rao (2004). *School Organisation*. New Delhi: Discovery Publishing House. ISBN 81-7141-843-0.

Ediger, Marlow and Digumarti Bhaskara Rao (2004). *Relevancy in Elementary Curriculum*. New Delhi: Discovery Publishing House. ISBN 81-7141-845-9.

Ediger, Marlow and Digumarti Bhaskara Rao (2005). *Quality School Education*. New Delhi: Discovery Publishing House. ISBN 81-8356-022-9.

Ediger, Marlow and Digumarti Bhaskara Rao (2006). *Successful School Education*. New Delhi: Discovery Publishing House. ISBN 81-8356-054-7.

Ediger, Marlow and Digumarti Bhaskara Rao (2006). *Successful School Administration*. New Delhi: Discovery Publishing House. ISBN 81-8356-046-6.

Ediger, Marlow and Digumarti Bhaskara Rao (2006). *Issues in School Curriculum*. New Delhi: Discovery Publishing House. ISBN 81-8356-052-0.

Ediger, Marlow and Digumarti Bhaskara Rao (2006). *Community College—Curriculum and Teaching*. New Delhi: Discovery Publishing House. ISBN 81-8356-053-9.

Ediger, Marlow and Digumarti Bhaskara Rao (2006). *Administration of Schools*. New Delhi: Discovery Publishing House. ISBN 81-8356-244-2.

Ediger, Marlow and Digumarti Bhaskara Rao (2006). *Reading Curriculum and Instruction*. New Delhi: Discovery Publishing House. ISBN 81-8356-266-3.

Ediger, Marlow and Digumarti Bhaskara Rao (2006). *Curriculum Organisation*. New Delhi: Discovery Publishing House. ISBN 81-8356-205-1.

Ediger, Marlow and Digumarti Bhaskara Rao (2006). *Curriculum of School Subjects*. New Delhi: Discovery Publishing House. ISBN 81-8356-207-8.

Ediger, Marlow, B.S.V. Dutt and Digumarti Bhaskara Rao (2003). *Teaching English Successfully*. New Delhi: Discovery Publishing House. ISBN 81-7141-707-8.

Ediger, Marlow and Digumarti Bhaskara Rao (2007). *School Science Education*. New Delhi: Discovery Publishing House. ISBN 81-8356-352-X.

Ediger, Marlow and Digumarti Bhaskara Rao (2007). *Language Arts Education*. New Delhi: Discovery Publishing House. ISBN 81-8356-333-3.

Ediger, Marlow and Digumarti Bhaskara Rao, Editors (2007). *Encyclopaedia of School Education*, 5 Volumes. New Delhi: Discovery Publishing House. ISBN 81-8356-308-6.

Ediger, Marlow and Digumarti Bhaskara Rao, Editors (2007). *Encyclopaedia of School Curriculum*, 10 Volumes. New Delhi: Discovery Publishing House. ISBN 81-8356-305-8.

Ediger, Marlow and Digumarti Bhaskara Rao, Editors (2007). *Encyclopaedia of School Administration*, 4 Volumes. New Delhi: Discovery Publishing House. ISBN 81-8356-307-4.

Elizabeth, M.E.S., Author and Digumarti Bhaskara Rao, Editor (2004). *Methods of Teaching English*. New Delhi: Discovery Publishing House. ISBN 81-7141-809-0.

Elizabeth, M.E.S., Author and Digumarti Bhaskara Rao, Editor (2004). *Acquisition of English Vocabulary*. New Delhi: Discovery Publishing House. ISBN 81-8356-075-X.

Fatima, Sk. Author and Digumarti Bhaskara Rao, Editor (2007). *Reasoning Ability of School Students*. New Delhi: Discovery Publishing House. ISBN 81-8356-330-9.

Fatima, Sk. and Digumarti Bhaskara Rao (2008). *Reasoning Ability of Adolescent Students*. New Delhi: Discovery Publishing House. ISBN 978-81-8356-315-4.

Gopala Krishna, M., Author and Digumarti Bhaskara Rao, Editor (2007). *Techniques of Teaching Physical Education*. New Delhi: Sonali Publications. ISBN 81-8411-044-8.

Gopala Krishna, M., Author and Digumarti Bhaskara Rao, Editor (2007). *Techniques of Teaching Education*. New Delhi: Sonali Publications. ISBN 81-8411-062-6.

Harshitha, Digumarthi, Author and Digumarti Bhaskara Rao, Editor (2004). *Methods of Teaching Information Technology*. New Delhi: Discovery Publishing House. ISBN 81-7141-805-8.

Harshitha, Digumarthi, Author and Digumarti Bhaskara Rao, Editor (2007). *Techniques of Teaching Computer Science*. New Delhi: Sonali Publications. ISBN 81-8411-036-7.

Indira Devi, Author and J. Prasanth Kumar and Digumarti Bhaskara Rao, Editors (2004). *Values in Language Text Books*. New Delhi: Discovery Publishing House. ISBN 81-7141-833-3.

Jalaja Kumari, C., Author and Digumarti Bhaskara Rao, Editor (2004). *Methods of Teaching Educational Technology*. New Delhi: Discovery Publishing House. ISBN 81-7141-810-4.

Jalaja Kumari, C., Author and Digumarti Bhaskara Rao, Editor (2007). *Job Satisfaction of Teachers*. New Delhi: Discovery Publishing House. ISBN 81-8356-329-5.

Janardhan Reddy, B., Author and Digumarti Bhaskara Rao, Editor (2006). *Techniques of Teaching Sociology*. New Delhi: Sonali Publications. ISBN 81-8411-042-1.

Jayalakshmi, M., Author and Digumarti Bhaskara Rao, Editor (2008). *Microteaching and Prospective Teachers*. New Delhi: Sonali Publications.

Jayasree, K., Author and Digumarti Bhaskara Rao, Editor (1999). *Correlates of Socialisation*. New Delhi: Discovery Publishing House. ISBN 81-7141-517-2.

Jayasree, K., Author and Digumarti Bhaskara Rao, Editor (2004). *Methods of Teaching Science*. New Delhi: Discovery Publishing House. ISBN 81-7141-801-5.

John Babu, C., Author and T.J.R. Prasad, G.M. Madhukar and Digumarti Bhaskara Rao, Editors (2004). *Problem Solving in Mathematics*. New Delhi: APH Publishing Corporation. ISBN 81-7648-273-0.

Joseph Raju, B and G.A. Anitha, Authors and Digumarti Bhaskara Rao, Editor (2004). *Population Education*. New Delhi: Sonali Publications. ISBN 81-88836-31-3.

Lalitha, T., Author and K.S. Prabhakaram, D.S.N. Sastry and Digumarti Bhaskara Rao, Editors (2004). *Educational Philosophic Beliefs*. New Delhi: Discovery Publishing House. ISBN 81-7141-765-5.

Krishna, G., Author and Digumarti Bhaskara Rao, Editor (2006). *Techniques of Teaching Physical Education*. New Delhi: Sonali Publications. ISBN 81-8411-044-8.

Kumar Raja, G., Author and Digumarti Bhaskara Rao, Editor (2007). *Principles of Primary School*. New Delhi: Sonali Publications. ISBN 81-8411-054-5.

Lakshmi Kumari, V., Author and Digumarti Bhaskara Rao, Editor (2006). *Techniques of Teaching Home Science*. New Delhi: Discovery Publishing House. ISBN 81-8411-048-0.

Madhava, K., Author and Digumarti Bhaskara Rao, Editor (2008). *Personality of Adolescent Students*. New Delhi: Discovery Publishing House. ISBN 978-81-8356-262-1.

Madhu Bala, Jampala, author and Digumarti Bhaskara Rao, Editor (2004). *Methods of Teaching Exceptional Children*. New Delhi: Discovery Publishing House. ISBN 81-7141-802-3.

Madhu Bala, Jampala, Author and Digumarti Bhaskara Rao, Editor (2004). *Adjustment Problems of Hearing Impaired*. New Delhi: Discovery Publishing House. ISBN 81 7141 831 7.

Marja, Talvi and Digumarti Bhaskara Rao, Editors (1996). *Educational Leadership and Social Changes*. New Delhi: Discovery Publishing House. ISBN 81-7141-320-X.

Mohana Sundari, C., Author and B. Prasad Babu and Digumarti Bhaskara Rao, Editors (2008). *Stress Among Pregnant Women* New Delhi: Discovery Publishing House. ISBN 978-81-8356-316-1.

Naga Kumari, U., Author and Digumarti Bhaskara Rao, Editor (2008). *Science Process Skills of School Students*. New Delhi: Discovery Publishing House Pvt. Ltd. ISBN 978-81-8356-263-8.

Nageswara Rao, S. and M. Srihari, Authors and Digumarti Bhaskara Rao, Editor (2004). *Guidance and Counselling*. New Delhi: Discovery Publishing House. ISBN 81-7141-840-6.

Nageswara Rao, S., Author and Digumarti Bhaskara Rao, Editor (2006). *Techniques of Teaching Psychology*. New Delhi: Discovery Publishing House. ISBN 81-8411-040-5.

Nageswara Rao, S. and P. Sridhar, Authors and Digumarti Bhaskara Rao, Editor (2004). *Methods and Techniques of Teaching*. New Delhi: Sonali Publications. ISBN 81-88836-33-8.

Nirmala Jyothi, M., Author and Digumarti Bhaskara Rao, Editor (2003). *Non-detention System in School Education*. New Delhi: Discovery Publishing House. ISBN 81-7141-654-3.

Padma Tulasi, G., Author and Digumarti Bhaskara Rao, Editor (2004). *Methods of Teaching Elementary Science*. New Delhi: Discovery Publishing House. ISBN 81-7141-871-6.

Pala Prasada Rao, V., Author and K.N. Rani and D. Bhaskara Rao, Editors (2004). India Pakistan: *Partition Perspectives in Indo English Novels*. New Delhi: Discovery Publishing House. ISBN 81-7141-871-6.

Pala Prasada Rao, V., Author and D. Bhaskara Rao, Editors (2008). *Functioning of Autonomous Colleges*. New Delhi: Discovery Publishing House Pvt. Ltd. ISBN 978-81-8356-258-4.

Pitchi Reddy, M., Author and Digumarti Bhaskara Rao, Editor (2007). *Techniques of Teaching Social Sciences*. New Delhi: Sonali Publications. ISBN 81-8411-066-X.

Prasad Babu, B., Author and P. Madhu and Digumarti Bhaskara Rao, Editors (2006). *Psychological Adjustment and Well-being*. New Delhi: Discovery Publishing House. ISBN 81-8356-204-3.

Prasad Babu, B., Author and M.V.R. Raju and Digumarti Bhaskara Rao, Editors (2006). *Behavioural Problems of School Children*. New Delhi: Discovery Publishing House. ISBN 81-8356-206-X.

Prabhakaram, K.S., Author and Digumarti Bhaskara Rao, Editors (1998). *Concept Attainment Model in Mathematics Teaching*. New Delhi: Discovery Publishing House. ISBN 81-7141-424-9.

Prasanth Kumar, J., Author and Digumarti Bhaskara Rao, Editor (1998). *Effectiveness of Distance Education System*. New Delhi: Discovery Publishing House. ISBN 81-7141-437-0.

Prasanth Kumar, J., Author and Digumarti Bhaskara Rao, Editor (2004). *Methods of Teaching Civics*. New Delhi: Discovery Publishing House. ISBN 81-7141-806-6.

Prasanth Kumar, J., Author and G. Sundara Rao and Digumarti Bhaskara Rao, Editors (2000). *Open University Student Support Services*. New Delhi: Discovery Publishing House. ISBN 81-7141-550-4.

Raja Kumari, M.A. and D.R.S. Sundari, Authors and Digumarti Bhaskara Rao, Editor (2004). *Special Education*. New Delhi: Discovery Publishing House. ISBN 81-7141-846-5.

Raja Kumari, M.A. and D.R.S. Sundari, Authors and Digumarti Bhaskara Rao, Editor (2004). *Methods of Teaching Educational Psychology*. New Delhi: Discovery Publishing House. ISBN 81-7141-820-1.

Rajeswari, S. M., Author and T. Santhanam, B. Prasad Babu and Digumarti Bhaskara Rao, Editors (2008). *Stress and Attitude of Women Teachers*. New Delhi: Discovery Publishing House Pvt. Ltd. ISBN 978-81-8356-324-6.

Ramatulasamma, K., Author and Digumarti Bhaskara Rao, Editor (2002). *Job Satisfaction of Teacher Educators*. New Delhi: Discovery Publishing House. ISBN 81-7141-655-1.

Rama Krishnaiah, D., Author and Digumarti Bhaskara Rao, Editor (1998). *Job Satisfaction of College Teachers*. New Delhi: Discovery Publishing House. ISBN 81-7141-438-9.

Rama Kumar Ratnam, M.V., Author and Digumarti Bhaskara Rao, Editor (1998). *Dukkha: Suffering in Early Buddhism*. New Delhi: Discovery Publishing House. ISBN 81-7141-653-5.

Rama Krishna Prasad and P. Vide Sagar, Authors and Digumarti Bhaskara Rao, Editor (2004). *Methods of Teaching Physical Education*. New Delhi: Discovery Publishing House. ISBN 81-7141-868-6.

Rama Seshaiah, P. Author and Digumarti Bhaskara Rao, Editor (2004). *Methods of Teaching Home Science*. New Delhi: Discovery Publishing House. ISBN 81-7141-916-X.

Rama Swamy, K., Author and Digumarti Bhaskara Rao, Editor (2007). *Techniques of Teaching Environmental Science*. New Delhi: Sonali Publications. ISBN 81-8411-035-9.

Ramesh, A.R., Author and Digumarti Bhaskara Rao, Editor (2006). *Techniques of Teaching Commerce*. New Delhi: Sonali Publications. ISBN 81-8411-043-X.

Ramesh, Ghanta and Digumarti Bhaskara Rao, Editors (1998). *Environmental Education: Problems and Prospects*. New Delhi: Discovery Publishing House. ISBN 81-7141-423-0.

Ranga Rao, B., Author and Digumarti Bhaskara Rao, Editor (2007). *Techniques of Teaching Economics*. New Delhi: Sonali Publications. ISBN 81-8411-056-1.

Ranga Rao, R., Author and Digumarti Bhaskara Rao, Editor (2004). *Methods of Teacher Teaching*. New Delhi: Discovery Publishing House. ISBN 81-7141-812-0.

Rani, S.S., Author and Digumarti Bhaskara Rao, Editor (2006). *Techniques of Teaching Botany*. New Delhi: Discovery Publishing House. ISBN 81-8411-037-5.

Rathaiah, Lavu and Digumarti Bhaskara Rao, Editors (1996), *International Innovations in Education*. New Delhi: Discovery Publishing House. ISBN 81-7141-359-5.

Rathaiah, Lavu and Digumarti Bhaskara Rao (1997). Achievement Correlates. New Delhi: Discovery Publishing House. ISBN 81-7141-385-4.

Ravi Krishna, M., Author and Digumarti Bhaskara Rao, Editor (2004). *Examination System*. New Delhi: Discovery Publishing House. ISBN 81-7141-824-4.

Ravi Kumar, M., Author and Digumarti Bhaskara Rao, editor (2004). *Methods of Teaching Computer Science*. New Delhi: Discovery Publishing House. ISBN 81-7141-823-6.

Roja Ramani, V., Author and Digumarti Bhaskara Rao, Editor (2008). *Frustration of Prospective Teachers*. New Delhi: Discovery Publishing House.

Rudramamba, B., Author and Digumarti Bhaskara Rao, Editor (2003). *Problems of Teaching*. New Delhi: APH Publishing Corporation. ISBN 81-7648-462-8.

Rudramamba, B. and V. Lakshmi Kumari, Authors and Digumarti Bhaskara Rao, Editor (2004). *Methods of Teaching Economics*. New Delhi: Discovery Publishing House. ISBN 81-7141-900-3.

Sambasiva Rao, P., Author and Digumarti Bhaskara Rao, Editor (2007). *Techniques of Teaching Psychology*. New Delhi: Sonali Publications. ISBN 81-8411-040-5.

Sanjeeva Rao, P.C., Author and Digumarti Bhaskara Rao, Editor (1996). *A Text Book of Geology*. New Delhi: Discovery Publishing House. ISBN 81-7141-313-7.

Santhanam, T., B. Prasad Babu and S. Sugandhi, Authors and Digumarti Bhaskara Rao, Editor (2007). *Children with Learning Disabilities*. New Delhi: Sonali Publications. ISBN 81-8411-077-4.

Santhanam, T., B. Prasad Babu and S. Sugandhi, Authors and Digumarti Bhaskara Rao, Editor (2008). *Learning Disabilities and Remedial Programmes*. New Delhi: Discovery Publishing House.

Sarala, M.M.O., Author and Digumarti Bhaskara Rao, Editor (2006). *Techniques of Teaching English*. New Delhi: Sonali Publications. ISBN 81-8411-047-2.

Satya Narayana, G., Author and Digumarti Bhaskara Rao, Editor (2008). *Attitude Towards Social Studies and Achievement in Social Studies*. New Delhi: Discovery Publishing House Pvt. Ltd. ISBN 978-81-8356-261-4.

Satya Narayana, V., Author and Digumarti Bhaskara Rao, Editor (2001). *Physical Education, Social Attitudes and Leadership Qualities*. New Delhi: Discovery Publishing House. ISBN 81-7141-593-8.

Satya Narayana, P.V.V. and G. Krishna, Authors and Digumarti Bhaskara Rao, Editor (2004). *Curriculum Development and Management*. New Delhi: Discovery Publishing House. ISBN 81-7141-813-9.

Shamsuddin, Sk. and V. Dayakara Reddy, Authors and Digumarti Bhaskara Rao, Editor (2007). *Values and Academic Achievement*. New Delhi: Discovery Publishing House. ISBN 81-8356-283-3.

Singh, Y.C., Author and Digumarti Bhaskara Rao, Editor (2006). *Techniques of Teaching Science*. New Delhi: Sonali Publications. ISBN 81-8411-041-3.

Sirisha Rani, S., Author and Digumarti Bhaskara Rao, Editor (2007). *Techniques of Teaching Botany*. New Delhi: Sonali Publications. ISBN 81-8411-037-5.

Sivaram Prasad, S., Author and Digumarti Bhaskara Rao, Editor (2009). *Creative Thinking of School Students*. New Delhi: Discovery Publishing House Pvt. Ltd.

Sivaratnam Reddy, M., Author and Digumarti Bhaskara Rao, Editor (2004). *Creativity in College Students*. New Delhi: Discovery Publishing House. ISBN 81-7141-697-7.

Siva Lakshmi, G.V. and G.L. Subbaiah, Authors and Digumarti Bhaskara Rao, Editor (2004). *Methods of Teaching Environmental Science*. New Delhi: Discovery Publishing House. ISBN 81-7141-839-2.

Srinivas, G. and Digumarti Bhaskara Rao (2007). *Anxiety of Prospective Teachers*. New Delhi: Sonali Publications. ISBN 81-8411-084-7.

Srinivas, M. and I. Prasada Rao, Authors and Digumarti Bhaskara Rao, Editor (2004). *Methods of Teaching History*. New Delhi: Discovery Publishing House. ISBN 81-7141-803-1.

Srinivas Rao, P., Author and Digumarti Bhaskara Rao, Editor (2007). *Principles of Secondary School*. New Delhi: Sonali Publications. ISBN 81-8411-058-8.

Srinivasulu Reddy, M. and K.R.S. Sambasiva Rao, Authors and Digumarti Bhaskara Rao, Editor (1999). *A Text Book of Aquaculture*. New Delhi: Discovery Publishing House. ISBN 81-7141-482-6.

Srinivasa Rao, Mandalapu, Author and Digumarti Bhaskara Rao, Editor (2003). *Achievement Motivation and Achievement in Mathematics*. New Delhi: Discovery Publishing House. ISBN 81-7141-674-8.

Srihari, M., Author and Digumarti Bhaskara Rao, Editor (2003). *Values of Prospective Teachers*. New Delhi: Discovery Publishing House. ISBN 81-8356-328-7.

Subba Rao, K., Author and Digumarti Bhaskara Rao, Editor (2007). *School Education Policy*. New Delhi: Discovery Publishing House. ISBN 81-8356-285-X.

Subba Rao, K., Author and Digumarti Bhaskara Rao, Editor (2007). *Educational Planning*. New Delhi: Sonali Publications. ISBN 81-8411-053-7.

Sudhakar Reddy, Y., Author and Digumarti Bhaskara Rao, Editor (2003). *Creativity in Adolescents*. New Delhi: Discovery Publishing House. ISBN 81-7141-659-4.

Sunil Kumar, K. and K. Rama Krishana, Authors and Digumarti Bhaskara Rao, Editor (2004). *Methods of Teaching Chemistry*. New Delhi: Discovery Publishing House. ISBN 81-7141-913-5.

Suneetha, G., Author and Digumarti Bhaskara Rao, Editor (2004). *Environmental Awareness of School Students*. New Delhi: Sonali Publications. ISBN 81-8411-085-5.

Sunita, E. and R. Sambasiva Rao, Authors and Digumarti Bhaskara Rao, Editor (2004). *Methods of Teaching Mathematics*. New Delhi: Discovery Publishing House. ISBN 81-7141-915-1.

Suresh, K., Author and Digumarti Bhaskara Rao, Editor (2008). *Social Intelligence of Prospective Teachers*. New Delhi: Sonali Publications.

Surya Madhava, I., Author and Digumarti Bhaskara Rao, Editor (2006). *Techniques of Teaching Geography*. New Delhi: Sonali Publications. ISBN 81-8411-034-0.

Surya Madhava, I., Author and Digumarti Bhaskara Rao, Editor (2007). *Techniques of Teaching Political Science*. New Delhi: Sonali Publications. ISBN 81-8411-061-8.

Suvarna Raju, T.J.M., Author and M.V.R. Raju, B. Prasad Babu and Digumarti Bhaskara Rao, Editors (2009). *Personality and Adjustment of University Hostel Students*. New Delhi: Discovery Publishing House Pvt. Ltd.

Swamy, K.R., Author and Digumarti Bhaskara Rao, Editor (2006). *Techniques of Teaching Environmental Science*. New Delhi: Sonali Publications. ISBN 81-8411-035-9.

Swarna Jyothi, K., Author and Digumarti Bhaskara Rao, Editor (2007). *Educational Research*. New Delhi: Sonali Publications. ISBN 81-8411-063-4.

Swarna Latha, C.D., and Digumarti Bhaskara Rao, Editors (2006). *Encyclopaedia of Biotechnology*, 5 Volumes. New Delhi: Discovery Publishing House. ISBN 81-8356-168-3.

Swarupa Rani, T. and J.R. Priyadarshini, Authors and Digumarti Bhaskara Rao, Editor (2004). *Educational Measurement and Evaluation*. New Delhi: Discovery Publishing House. ISBN 81-7141-859-7.

Vanaja, M., Author and Digumarti Bhaskara Rao, Editor (1999). *Inquiry Training Model*. New Delhi: Discovery Publishing House. ISBN 81-7141-515-6.

Vanaja, M., Author and Digumarti Bhaskara Rao, Editor (2004). *Methods of Teaching Physics*. New Delhi: Discovery Publishing House. ISBN 81-7141-867-8.

Valeri V. Koustiouk, Author and Digumarti Bhaskara Rao, Editor (2002). *A Text Book of Cryogenics*. New Delhi: Discovery Publishing House. ISBN 81-7141-642-X.

Vamsi Krishna, V., Author and Digumarti Bhaskara Rao, Editor (2004). *School Psychology*. New Delhi: Discovery Publishing House. ISBN 81-7141-880-5.

Veena Kumari, Balusu and Digumarti Bhaskara Rao (1996). *Operation Black Board*. New Delhi: APH Publishing Corporation. ISBN 81-7024-711-X.

Veena Kumari, Balusu, Author and Digumarti Bhaskara Rao, Editor (2004). *Methods of Teaching Social Studies*. New Delhi: Discovery Publishing House. ISBN 81-7141-899-6.

Veena Kumari, Balusu, Author and Digumarti Bhaskara Rao, Editor (2000). *Psycho-Social Correlates of Achievement*. New Delhi: Discovery Publishing House. ISBN 81-7141-547-4.

Venkata Rao, B., Author and Digumarti Bhaskara Rao, Editor (2007). *Techniques of Teaching Chemistry*. New Delhi: Sonali Publications. ISBN 81-8411-057-X.

Venkata Rao, P. and Digumarti Bhaskara Rao (1989). *A Text Book of Zoology—Junior Intermediate*. Guntur: Vignan Publishers.

Venkata Rao, P. and Digumarti Bhaskara Rao (1989). *A Text Book of Zoology—Senior Intermediate*. Guntur: Vignan Publishers.

Venkateswara Rao, V., Author and Digumarti Bhaskara Rao, Editor (2004). *Problems of Education*. New Delhi: Discovery Publishing House. ISBN 81-7141-841-4.

Venkateswara Rao, V., V. Vijaya Lakshmi and V. Vamsi Krishna, Authors and Digumarti Bhaskara Rao, Editor (2004). *Education For All*. New Delhi: Sonali Publications. ISBN 81-88836-30-3.

Venkateswara Rao, V., V. Vijaya Lakshmi and V. Vamsi Krishna, Authors and Digumarti Bhaskara Rao, Editor (2004). *Education in India*. New Delhi: Sonali Publications. ISBN 81-88836-858-9.

Venkateswara Reddy, L. and Narayana, M. L., Authors and Digumarti Bhaskara Rao, Editor (2004). *Education for Dalits*. New Delhi: Discovery Publishing House. ISBN 81-7141-872-4.

Venkateswara Reddy, L. and Narayana, M.L, Authors and Digumarti Bhaskara Rao, Editor (2004). *Methods of Teaching Rural Sociology*. New Delhi: Discovery Publishing House. ISBN 81-7141-811-2.

Venkateswarlu, K. and S.J. Basha, Authors and Digumarti Bhaskara Rao, Editor (2004). *Methods of Teaching Commerce*. New Delhi: Discovery Publishing House. ISBN 81-7141-808-2.

Venugopala Rao, K., Author and Digumarti Bhaskara Rao, Editor (2000). *Teacher Morale in Secondary Schools*. New Delhi: Discovery Publishing House. ISBN 81-7141-551-2.

Venugopala Rao, K., Author and Digumarti Bhaskara Rao, Editor (2007). *Techniques of Teaching History*. New Delhi: Sonali Publications. ISBN 81-8411-059-6.

Vidya, C., Author and Digumarti Bhaskara Rao, Editor (1996). *A Text Book of Nutrition*. New Delhi: Discovery Publishing House. ISBN 81-7141-309-9.

Vimala, T.D., B. Prasad Babu and Digumarti Bhaskara Rao, Editors (2007). *Stress, Coping and Management*. New Delhi: Sonali Publications. ISBN 81-8411-086-3.

Vijaya Bharathi, D., Author and Digumarti Bhaskara Rao, Editor (2000). *Educational Philosophies of Swami Vivekananda and John Dewey*. New Delhi: APH Publishing House. ISBN 81-7648-309-9.

Vijaya Bharathi, D., Author and Digumarti Bhaskara Rao, Editor (2005). *Educational Philosophy of John Dewey*. New Delhi: Discovery Publishing House. ISBN 81-8356-024-5.

Vijaya Bharathi, D., Author and Digumarti Bhaskara Rao, Editor (2005). *Educational Philosophy of Swami Vivekananda*. New Delhi: Discovery Publishing House. ISBN 81-8356-023-7.

Vijaya Lakshmi, D., Author and Digumarti Bhaskara Rao, Editor (2004) *Basic Education*. New Delhi: Discovery Publishing House. ISBN 81-7141-881-3.

Vijaya Lakshmi, V., Author and Digumarti Bhaskara Rao, Editor (2006). *Techniques of Teaching Music*. New Delhi: Sonali Publications. ISBN 81-8411-038-3.

Vijaya Kumar, S.J., Author and Digumarti Bhaskara Rao, Editor (2006). *Techniques of Teaching Mathematics*. New Delhi: Sonali Publications. ISBN 81-8411-039-1.

Visalakshi, V., Author and Digumarti Bhaskara Rao, Editor (2006). *Techniques of Teaching Biology*. New Delhi: Sonali Publications. ISBN 81-8411-045-6.

Visalakshi, V., Author and Digumarti Bhaskara Rao, Editor (2007). *Techniques of Teaching Zoology*. New Delhi: Sonali Publications. ISBN 81-8411-055-3.

Bhaskara Rao, Digumarti (1986). *Dhrushya Sravana Bodhanapakaranalu* (Audio-visual Teaching Aids). Guntur: Nagarjuna Publishers.

Bhaskara Rao, Digumarti (1993). *Jeevasashtra Bodhana* (Teaching of Biology). Guntur: Nagarjuna Publishers.

Bhaskara Rao, Digumarti (1995). *Vignanasasthra Bodhana* (Teaching of Science) Guntur: Nagarjuna Publishers.

Bhaskara Rao, Digumarti (1997). *Vidya Manovignana Sastram* (Educational Psychology). Guntur: Creative Press.

Bhaskara Rao, Digumarti (1998). *DSC Study Material*. Guntur: Nagarjuna Publishers.

Bhaskara Rao, Digumarti (1998). *Upadhyayudu Vidya*. (Teacher and Education) Guntur: Nagarjuna Publishers.

Bhaskara Rao, Digumarti (1998). *Vidya Drukpadalu* (Perspectives of Education). Guntur: Nagarjuna Publishers.

Bhaskara Rao, Digumarti (1999). *EdCET Teaching Aptitude*. Guntur: Nagarjuna Publishers.

Bhaskara Rao, Digumarti (2001). *Bharata Samajamulo Upadyayudu Vidhya* (Teacher and Education in Emerging Indian Society). Guntur: Sri Nagarjuna Publishers.

Bhaskara Rao, Digumarti (2001). *Bhoutika Sastra Bodhana Padhatulu* (Methods of Teaching Physical Science). Guntur: Sri Nagarjuna Publishers.

Bhaskara Rao, Digumarti (2001). *Jeeva Sastra Bodhana Padhatulu* (Methods of Teaching Biology).Guntur: Sri Nagarjuna Publishers.

Bhaskara Rao, Digumarti (2001). *Vidya Manovignana Sastram* (Educational Psychology). Guntur: Sri Nagarjuna Publishers.

Bhaskara Rao, Digumarti (2003). Patasala Yajamanyam/ Paripalana (School Management and Administration). Guntur: Sri Nagarjuna Publishers.

Gopala Krishna, G., A. Rama Krishna, K. Subba Rao and Bhaskara Rao, Digumarti (2004). *Jeevasashtra Bodhana Padhatulu* (Methods of Teaching of Biological Science). Guntur: Sri Nagarjuna Publishers.

Krishna Murthy, V., K.S. Sudheer Reddy and Digumarti Bhaskara Rao (2004). *Vidya Manovignana Sastra Adharalu* (Foundations of Educational Psychology). Guntur: Sri Nagarjuna Publishers.

Lalini, V., V. Dayakara Reddy, M. Srihari and Digumarti Bhaskara Rao (2004). *Vidya Adharalu* (Foundations of Education). Guntur: Sri Nagarjuna Publishers.

Subba Rao, K.P., P. Ayodhya and Digumarti Bhaskara Rao (2004). *Patasala Yajamanyam – Vidhya Vyavasthalu* (School Management and Systems of Education). Guntur: Sri Nagarjuna Publishers.

Sudhakar, V., B. Ravindra Babu, D.S. Kumar and Digumarti Bhaskara Rao (2004). *Vidya Sanketika Sastram—Computer Vidhya* (Educational Technology and Computer Education). Guntur: Sri Nagarjuna Publishers.

Index

❑❑❑